# NO TIME FOR SERGEANTS

# No
# Time
# for

# Sergeants

*by*
## IRA LEVIN
*(Adapted from the novel by MAC HYMAN)*

 *Random House, New York*

FIRST PRINTING

Photographs by courtesy of Fred Fehl

Library of Congress Catalog Card Number: 56-6712

MANUFACTURED IN THE UNITED STATES OF AMERICA

No Time for Sergeants *was presented by Maurice Evans, in association with Emmett Rogers, at the Alvin Theatre, New York City, October 20, 1955, with the following cast:*

(IN ORDER OF APPEARANCE)

| | |
|---|---|
| PREACHER | Don Knotts |
| WILL STOCKDALE | Andy Griffith |
| PA STOCKDALE | Floyd Buckley |
| DRAFT MAN | O. Tolbert-Hewitt |
| BUS DRIVER | Michael Thoma |
| IRVIN BLANCHARD | Robert Webber |
| ROSABELLE | Maree Dow |
| INDUCTEES | Cecil Rutherford<br>Robert McQuade<br>Carl Albertson<br>Arthur P. Keegan<br>Van Williams<br>Jules Racine<br>Wynn Pearce |
| BEN WHITLEDGE | Roddy McDowall |
| SERGEANT KING | Myron McCormick |
| A CAPTAIN | Ed Peck |
| A NURSE | Maree Dow |
| FIRST CLASSIFICATION CORPORAL | Robert McQuade |
| SECOND CLASSIFICATION CORPORAL | Don Knotts |
| THIRD CLASSIFICATION CORPORAL | Ray Johnson |

| | |
|---|---|
| A LIEUTENANT | Earle Hyman |
| A PSYCHIATRIST | James Millhollin |
| CIGARETTE GIRL | Maree Dow |
| AN INFANTRYMAN | Arthur P. Keegan |
| AIR FORCE POLICEMAN | Jules Racine |
| A COLONEL | Rex Everhart |
| LT. BRIDGES (PILOT) | Hazen Gifford |
| LT. GARDELLA (CO-PILOT) | Carl Albertson |
| LT. KENDALL (ENGINEER) | Cecil Rutherford |
| LT. COVER (NAVIGATOR) | Bill Hinnant |
| GENERAL BUSH | Howard Freeman |
| GENERAL POLLARD | Royal Beal |
| A SENATOR | O. Tolbert-Hewitt |
| AIDE TO GENERAL POLLARD | Ray Johnson |
| LT. ABEL | Rex Everhart |
| LT. BAKER | Edmund Johnston |
| CAPT. CHARLES | Wynn Pearce |

*Production directed by* Morton Da Costa

*Sets designed by* Peter Larkin

*Costumes by* Noel Taylor

*Lighting by* Peggy Clark

The action of the play takes place in and above the United States of America. Some of it is happening now and some of it happened a while back. There are two acts.

# ACT ONE

# ACT ONE

*The house curtain rises on a second curtain, that of the "Callville Township Meeting Hall," on which is depicted a horde of Confederate soldiers surging on toward victory. The house lights dim, amateur musicians are heard, and the* PREACHER *enters from the wings, applauding solicitously.*

### PREACHER
Thank you, members of the Civic Orchestra, for fillin' in so beautifully, but now our speaker has finally arrived. And here he is, Callville's favorite son in uniform—Will Stockdale. (*He motions toward the wings, coaxes applause from audience—but no one appears*) Will Stockdale!

> (WILL STOCKDALE *enters, wearing a private's uniform. He watches the* PREACHER *exit, then finds the mark at the center of the stage and faces the audience. He would rather be anywhere else in the world.*)

### WILL
Howdy. How I Won My Medal. (*Pause*) There's this medal that I got in the draft and I'm supposed to tell you how I won it. Well I didn't *win* it exactly; more like this fellow just *slipped* it to me. I tell you the truth, I'd just as soon somebody come up here and sung a song or somethin'. (*He heads for the wings, stops, nods obediently several times and returns to center stage*) Well, How I Won My Medal. The whole thing begun, of course, when I went into the draft. Well, I didn't

3

exactly *go in* to the draft, neither. What it was, was the draft *come out* to me. Last spring that was, one evenin' around the time the chickens was quietin' down. You know. (*Through the "Meeting Hall" curtain, a ramshackle cabin is seen, surrounded by scrubby trees.* PA STOCKDALE *is sitting on the porch steps, his chin in his hands, angry-looking. An ancient radio on a shelf is straining out hillbilly music. A rifle is propped against the front of the cabin; near it, a sleeping hound-dog whose head droops over the edge of the porch*) Pa and I had gone fishin' that day and he was settin' on the front steps of our place with his neck all red and his foot tappin'— angry, kind of. I'd caught a bigger fish than him. Anyhow, things was right peaceful, with my dog Blue asleep there, and the radio playin' some good music and all. (PA *has heard something. He stands and looks off right*) And then, all of a sudden, Pa stood up. Now that surprised me a good bit right there, because usually when we go fishin' it takes Pa two-three hours to get over it.

PA

(*Calling, still looking off*)

Will!

(*"Meeting Hall" curtain rises as* WILL *turns upstage.*)

WILL

What is it, Pa?
(*Starts to undo his tie.*)

PA

Come over here!
(WILL *heads for porch, taking off tie.*)

**4**

**WILL**
*(To audience)*
I warn't in uniform then.
*(Goes up to PA, unbuttoning shirt.)*

**PA**
Listen. Your ears are better than mine. Somebody's comin'.

**WILL**
I don't hear nothin'.

**PA**
Turn off that whatchamacallit.

**WILL**
Radio.

**PA**
I know what you call it. Turn it off. (WILL *turns it off, drops shirt and tie on porch. He is now in T-shirt and khaki trousers*) First I heared one of them cars, and then it stopped, and now somebody's comin'. *(Sound of twigs breaking and mumbled cursing off right)* Hear?

**DRAFT MAN**
*(Off)*
You stay right here and if I call come a'running.
*(PA snatches up rifle, holds it ready.)*

**WILL**
*(Trying to restrain him)*
Pa . . . That ain't no way to welcome folks. Maybe it's kin.

**5**

PA

Kin don't come in cars. See if you can wake that hound-dog.

WILL

(*Crouching beside dog*)

Hey, Blue. C'mon Blue. Got a big old hambone for you. C'mon Blue . . .

(*Approaching sounds have been growing louder. Now* DRAFT MAN *comes bursting in; a short, fat man in a white linen suit. He is sweating, fuming, and picking branches from his ankles.*)

DRAFT MAN

Never seen such a prickly path in all my whole life! . . . Damn! (*Coming up for air before* WILL, *who is still crouching*) You Will Stockdale?

WILL

(*Rising*)

Howdy . . .

DRAFT MAN

(*Pointing vigorously*)

Three damn times I been out here this month!

PA

(*Raising rifle*)

Don't you pint your finger in my boy's face!

DRAFT MAN

(*Retreating a step*)

Are you threatening me with a firearm? I'm a government representative on government business!

6

PA

Bustin' up here without sayin' Howdy or nothin' . . .
What government?

DRAFT MAN

U.S. Government! The draft board! This boy's been called
for the April draft and never reported. He's a draft-dodger!
(*He points again.*)

PA

Fold in that finger, sir! I'm warnin' you, fold in that finger!

DRAFT MAN
(*Lowering his hand*)
He can be put in jail for that. He's in tomorrow's group.
(*Turning to Will*) This is your last chance, and by God, if you
don't leave with that group at seven A.M. you're gonna be in
more trouble than you ever seen! You already got one offense
against you for not answering my letters!

WILL

I never got no letters.

DRAFT MAN

And don't tell me you can't read because you could've got
somebody to read 'em to you, so that ain't no excuse!
(WILL, *shocked, turns to* PA.)

PA

Do you mean to stand here and say to my face that my son
can't read?

DRAFT MAN

Now look . . .

7

PA

Do you think my son, who has *gone to school* and who has read *more times* than you could shake a stick at, couldn't read a puny little ole letter if he wanted to? By God, sir!

WILL

I never *got* no letters.

PA

I don't think I can stand to *listen* to any more of this, by God! Get that book! (WILL *exits into cabin. To* DRAFT MAN) No sir! What you think don't mean nothin' to me . . . (*Levels rifle again*) But we're gonna settle this here question here and now, and not have no more foolishness about it! (WILL *enters from cabin with book*) Read at 'im!

WILL

(*Clears throat. Reads slowly*)

Once there was a boy named Tony who wanted a pony. He went to his Mama and said, "May I have a pony?" and his Mama said, (*Turns page*) "No, Tony, you may not have a pony." (*Looks at* PA, *who signals him to continue*) So he went to his Papa and said, "May I have a pony?" and his Papa said, "No, Tony, you may not have—(*Turns page*)—a pony." (PA *lifts hand grandly.* WILL *closes book. To* DRAFT MAN:) End of the book, he gets the pony anyhow.

PA

(*Advancing on* DRAFT MAN)

Now that we've settled whether or not my boy can read . . .

WILL

Pa . . .

PA

. . . you best be gettin' off'n my property and into that car of yourn and out of range of—

WILL

Pa . . . Be Christian to him.

PA

Christian? You know what Christ woulda done if a man come stompin' onto *His* property . . . not sayin' Howdy or nothin' . . . sayin' folks couldn't read? *I* know what He woulda done. He woulda sent that man straight to *hell,* by God!

WILL

Pa! (*Taking* PA's *shoulder, gently*) Now, I want to talk to you for a minute. Come here. (PA *turns to* WILL, *who backs toward cabin.* PA *looks back at* DRAFT MAN, *lowers rifle reluctantly and joins* WILL. *They sit on porch steps*) Now, Pa, listen. I don't think this here draft is such a bad idea. I mean, I'd kind of like to go. There's a whole bunch of fellows there and they all march along right snappy-like—

PA

You listen to me, boy. Goin' into the draft don't mean just goin' into town. It means Macon and Atlanta, and farther still. I been to Atlanta—you know that—when I was no older than you. I told you how them folks . . . laughed at me and called me smart names. You don't want that, boy.

WILL

Pa, now ain't the same as it was then.

**9**

PA

The hell it ain't.

WILL

But they *want* me. They even sent a man to come and fetch me, didn't they? And that ain't all. Last spring I seen this sign out on the sidewalk down there in town. This big picture of Uncle Sam. And "*Uncle Sam* wants you," he's sayin'—just like this fellow here, Pa, pintin' straight in my face. And don't you think this soldier fellow come up to me right then and there, invitin' me to come along with all the other fellows? I told him how you was ailin' then and would he kindly wait a while. (*Pause*) You been tearin' up them letters, haven't you, Pa? And you ain't ailin' no more. (*He rises*) Say good-bye to Blue for me when he wakes up, will you?

(*Holds out his hand.*)

PA

You'll see, thing's ain't no different. They'll make fun of you . . . and talk sassy 'cause you ain't a town boy . . . (*Rises, grabs* WILL's *hand*) Write to me regular, you hear?

WILL

Sure, Pa.
(WILL *backs toward* DRAFT MAN.)

PA

Print big!

DRAFT MAN

All right now . . .

PA

Draft man! You tell them folks out there to be nice to that
boy, hear? (DRAFT MAN *mutters an impatient affirmative*)
He's a *good* boy. And it's my fault he didn't come when he
should'a.

(WILL *and* DRAFT MAN *start off.*)

DRAFT MAN

Yeah, yeah . . .

WILL

'Bye, Pa.

PA

'Bye, Will . . . (*He picks up "Tony and The Pony," holds it
out*) You want your book?

WILL

No, Pa . . . 'Bye.

(PA *watches them off, looks at book, wipes it slowly
with his sleeve. The lights dim out.*)

(*Lights come up on the town square. A bus stands
upstage. There is a statue at stage right and a gas
station with two pumps at stage left.* INDUCTEES *are
lounging around; one strumming a guitar and singing
softly, one embracing a girl. As more* INDUCTEES *drift
in, a civilian* BUS DRIVER *takes forms which they carry
and gives them blue cards in exchange.*)

DRIVER

Fill it out. Last name first, first name, middle name last.
(*Gives a card to another* INDUCTEE) Fill it out. Last name first,
first name, middle name last.

(IRVIN BLANCHARD *enters, wearing a leather jacket and dark glasses. He looks about disdainfully.*)

#### IRVIN

This the group going to the Air Force?

#### DRIVER

That's where I'm driving the bus to. You want me to reserve you a seat?

#### IRVIN

All right, save the jokes for the plowboys.

#### DRIVER

(*Glaring at* IRVIN, *giving him card*)
Fill it out. Last name first, first name, middle name last.

#### IRVIN

I know.
(IRVIN *moves aside and begins writing as* DRAFT MAN *enters, his right wrist handcuffed to* WILL's *left.*)

#### DRAFT MAN

Stand back, everybody. Stand back. Don't come too close. Keep away from him. (INDUCTEES *who have been lying down, sit up. Guitar stops.* WILL *looks shamefaced as* DRAFT MAN *transfers cuff from his own wrist to gas pump*) Reckon this'll hold you.

#### WILL

Yes, sir.

**DRIVER**

Have any trouble bringing him over, Mr. McKinney?

**DRAFT MAN**

(*Finished with handcuffs, stepping back and surveying* WILL)
Uh-uh. Night in jail simmered all the wildness out of him.
(*Takes forms and cards from* DRIVER. DRAFT MAN *gives card
and pencil to* WILL) Fill it out. Last name first, first name,
middle name last. Lean on the pump there.

**WILL**

Last name first . . .

**DRAFT MAN**

First name, middle name last. (WILL, *looking confused,
holds card against pump and begins to write.*) Any of you
boys had any R.O.T.C.?

**IRVIN**

I did. Close to a year.

**DRAFT MAN**

What's your name?

**IRVIN**

Blanchard, Irvin S.

**DRAFT MAN**

Okay, Irvin, I'm setting you in charge of the group. When
the bus gets to the Classification Center, report to the Sergeant there. Give him these here forms.

**IRVIN**

(*Nodding toward* WILL)
What about *him*?

DRAFT MAN

Better keep the cuffs on him. Here's the key. It took me two months to flush him out of the hills, so see that he don't get away.

DRIVER

Mr. McKinney . . .

(DRAFT MAN *goes over to* DRIVER. IRVIN *goes to* WILL.)

IRVIN

You hear what he said, plowboy? I don't want any trouble, you understand?

WILL

Oh, me neither, Irvin.

IRVIN

My name to you is Blanchard.

WILL

(*Extending his hand*)

It's a real pleasure.

IRVIN

Are you getting smart with me, plowboy? (WILL *shakes his head*) I don't want to hear one peep out of you. Not a peep!

(IRVIN *moves aside.* WILL *resumes writing.*)

DRAFT MAN

All right, boys. Irvin here is in charge. Do like he tells you and don't give him any trouble. Callville is proud of her sons in uniform. Show them what kind of men we raise down here. Be good, and if you can't be good, be careful. (*He laughs up-*

*roariously at his joke, then catches sight of the* INDUCTEE *and* GIRL *embracing by bus*) Rosabelle!

ROSABELLE
(*Breaking away from the* INDUCTEE)
Pa!

DRAFT MAN
Get on home!

ROSABELLE
Yes, Pa!
(*She runs off.*)

DRAFT MAN
I told you to stay home this time. Now git! Ma'll kill you! (*To* INDUCTEES) Well, 'bye, boys. Don't take any wooden nickels!
(*This line really kills him. He exits in a roar of laughter, which is echoed mockingly by the* INDUCTEES. IRVIN *moves to center and silences them.*)

IRVIN
Okay. Okay! Into the bus when I call your name. DeRoy, Richard S.

FIRST INDUCTEE
Here!
(*Gives card to* IRVIN *and exits around bus. Other* INDUCTEES *do the same when their names are called.*)

IRVIN
Farnum, Robert E.

SECOND INDUCTEE

Here!

IRVIN

Hooper, Junior C.

THIRD INDUCTEE

Here!

IRVIN

Lemon, Henry P.

FOURTH INDUCTEE

Here!

IRVIN

Stockdale, Will.

WILL

*(Pause)*

Here . . .

IRVIN

Swinburne, Armand A.

FIFTH INDUCTEE

Here!

IRVIN

Whitledge, Benjamin B. *(Pause)* Whitledge, Benjamin B.!
(WHITLEDGE, BENJAMIN B., *comes running in, an overnight bag in one hand, a pink envelope in the other. He is small, spindly and frenetic.*)

16

BEN

Here! Here! Whitledge! Here! Benjamin B.! Is Mr. McKinney here? Mr. McKinney—the man on the draft board! Where is he?

IRVIN

Who?

BEN

Mr. McKinney, the man on the draft board! Where'd he go? I got a letter for him!

IRVIN

Take it easy, sonny. You just missed him.

BEN

I got to find him! I got a letter for him!

IRVIN

He left *me* in charge.
        (*Plucks the letter out of* BEN's *hand.*)

BEN

Hey, give me that! That's a private letter! You can't take that! It's official business, for Mr. McKinney! Give it back!
        (IRVIN *pushes* BEN *away from him roughly.* WILL *extends his free arm and keeps* BEN *from falling over backwards.*)

IRVIN

Don't you understand English? *I'm* in charge. (*Shoves card at* BEN) Fill out this card.

BEN

That's a private letter . . . (IRVIN *glares at him, moving upstage*) You big . . .

WILL

Don't get sore at Irvin, fellow. He's had R.O.T.C.

BEN

That don't give him no right to push me around.
(*Starts to fill out card.*)

WILL

You put your last name, and then your first name, and then . . . (*Shows his card to* BEN) Like this.

BEN
(*Reading*)
Stockdale, Will, Will, Stockdale, Stockdale, Stockdale . . .
(*Shaking head*) All you need is one of each.

WILL

That's all?
(*Scratches head, begins crossing out extra names.*)

BEN
(*Glaring toward* IRVIN)
Wise guy . . .
(WILL *drops pencil, has difficulty retrieving it because of handcuffs,* BEN *picks it up for him, notices handcuffs.*)

BEN

What's the matter with you?

18

WILL

They think I'm a draft-dodger, but I ain't.

BEN

(*Taking* WILL's *card*)

Here, give me . . . You can't write good with handcuffs.

WILL

Thanks. Can't write much good *without* 'em, neither.

BEN

(*Glares at* IRVIN)

Big shot! (*To* WILL) Ever have measles?

WILL

No.

BEN

(*Making checks on card*)

The mumps?

WILL

No.

BEN

Chicken pox . . .

WILL

No.

BEN

Any other communicable diseases?

WILL

Reckon not. (*Watches* BEN *write*) You figger they're gonna make me go back home?

IRVIN

(*Reading letter*)
Hey Wiggins, come here!
(INDUCTEE *comes to* IRVIN, *reads over his shoulder.*)

BEN

Ever break any bones?

WILL

Leg bone once.

BEN

Which leg?

WILL

The right. No, it was the left. Yeh, the left.

BEN

(*Writing*)
Any member of your family belong to groups planning to overthrow the government by unconstitutional means?

WILL

(*Thinks*)
No, we're pretty satisfied. (BEN *writes.* WILL *thinks*) He still limps a mite.

BEN

Who does?

20

WILL

That fellow whose leg bone I broke. (BEN *looks annoyedly at* WILL, *begins erasing*) He hit me first . . .

WIGGINS

Hey, Young!
(*Another* INDUCTEE *joins* IRVIN *and* WIGGINS. *They chuckle over the letter.*)

BEN

Did you ever have R.O.T.C.?

WILL

No. (*Pause*) Irvin had it—close to a year. I figure he still got a touch of it in him.

BEN

Look, Stockdale—

WILL

Will's my name.

BEN

Listen . . .

WILL

What's yours again?

BEN

Ben Whitledge.

WILL

Howdy.
(*He extends his hand.* BEN *shakes it.*)

21

**BEN**

Hi. Look, Will, R.O.T.C. ain't a disease. It's training. Reserve, Officer, Training—uh—Corporation.

**WILL**

Is that the truth . . .

**BEN**

Sure. There's different kinds. There's Cavalry R.O.T.C., Artillery R.O.T.C., Infantry R.O.T.C. . . . Infantry's the best

**WILL**

Yeah . . that's what I always thought . . . (BEN *writes on his own card*) Ben, Irvin ain't sick?

**BEN**

No. And he don't rank no higher than we do, neither, 'cause R.O.T.C. don't mean nothing unless you finish the course.

**IRVIN**

(*Removing glasses and holding up sheet of pink paper*)
"So I beg of you, Mr. McKinney, please get my enclosed letter to the Commanding Officer in the Air Force."

**BEN**

Hey, you . . .
(BEN *flies at* IRVIN *but* WIGGINS *and* YOUNG *grab him.*)

**IRVIN**

". . . so that my son Ben will be put into the Infantry the same as his six brothers . . ."

22

**BEN**

Give me that! You big—let go! Let go of me!

**IRVIN**

"All his life little Ben has been dreaming of being a real Infantry soldier like all the men in our family." (INDUCTEES *roar*) Little Ben wanna be a big soldier!

**WILL**

(*Loud. Silencing them*)
Irvin! That there letter belongs to Ben. You give it to him.

**IRVIN**

I told you to keep your mouth shut, plowboy! (*Resumes reading*) "It will break his poor heart if he's put in the Air Force instead of—"

(WILL *wrenches his arm free, along with a piece of the gas pump.*)

**WILL**

Give Ben his letter, Irvin.

**IRVIN**

(*A bit pale*)
I'm in charge here . . . I'm warning you . . .

**WILL**

Ben, are you absolutely sure about that R.O.T.C.? (BEN, *still held captive, nods,* WILL *hits* IRVIN; *a blockbuster. As* IRVIN *collapses,* WILL *plucks the letter out of his hand and gives it to* BEN. *Light irises down to a pin-spot on* WILL. *He turns, comes downstage and addresses audience, attempting to conceal the handcuffs, which embarrass him.*) After laying there in that jail till seven o'clock in the morning it was right good to finally git some exercise. Well anyhow, we had a real nice ride up to the Classification Center. Ben and I got us a seat in the back of the bus and what we done was every fifteen minutes we switched around—you know, so there wouldn't be neither one of us settin' next to the window no longer than the other. We rode up through Pinehurst, and then another town just as big, and then another town as big as Pinehurst and Callville put together! You never seen nothin' like it. And then we come to Macon. Whew! Half an hour to get through it! And it was real fun, with all the fellows hangin' out the bus windows, whistlin' at the gals and hollerin' "Oh, you kid" and "I want you in my stockin' for Christmas" and a whole lot of funny sayings like that. I did enjoy it that day. But somewhere between Macon and Atlanta, Ben and I both dozed off and didn't wake up until we was at the Classification Center.

(*Lights fade on him. Whistle blows in darkness. Light comes up on* SERGEANT KING, *standing before a section of wall on which is a bulletin board marked "Barracks #10—Sgt. King." KING looks very tired and somewhat pained by it all. He gives another blast on the whistle.*)

KING

Please . . . let's keep it quiet . . . (*He waits for silence, glances at his wrist watch, and starts unreeling his orientation speech in a somnambulistic monotone, avoiding any inflection that might give meaning to the words. He takes a breath whenever he feels the need—usually in mid-sentence*) On behalf of the President of the United States, the Secretary of the Air Force and the Commanders of the base and this squadron, I want to welcome you gentlemen to the United States Air Force. This is a classification center where you will undergo a series of tests both physical and mental designed to determine your abilities and potentialities so that you may be trained for the position from which you and the Air Force will derive the greatest benefit, tests are for your own good so do your best in every test. My name is King, K-I-N-G, *Sergeant* King, and I'm in charge of this barracks in which you will be billeted for approximately two weeks. During this period the barracks *will* be kept spotlessly clean, maybe it's just a stopping place to you, but to me—*it's home.* Before turning in tonight every one of you will write a letter to your nearest of kin informing them that you have arrived safely and *are in the best of health.* If at any time a problem should arise, feel free to consult me about its solution. (*Opens door of his room*) I am here to help you during these first difficult days of military service. *Knock before entering.*

(*He exits, closing door. Blackout. Lights come up in* KING's *room, a cosy place with many homelike touches.* KING *stands just within door, garrison cap in hand, wiping his forehead. He hangs cap on hook, goes to radio on shelf and turns it on. Pausing to straighten framed sampler on which "Mother" is embroidered in prominent letters, he goes down to small table with hotplate and percolator.* KING *jiggles percolator, nods, sets it on hotplate, flicks switch, and looks at his watch. Knock on door.*)

KING

Come in.

(IRVIN *enters, still in civilian clothes, holding the forms that* DRAFT MAN *gave him. He comes to attention.*)

IRVIN

Private Blanchard delivering forms on eight inductees as ordered.

KING

(*A contemplative pause*)
You keep standing like that, you're gonna pull a muscle. (*Starts taking off tie*) Just put them down. (IRVIN *starts to put forms on bunk*) Not on the bed please. (IRVIN *looks around for someplace else.* KING *nods toward the table.* IRVIN *puts forms there, hesitates*) Anything else?

IRVIN

Sergeant, I feel it's my duty to tell you about one of the men. Fellow named Stockdale. A draft-dodger. He gave me a lot of trouble. (*Takes handcuffs out of pocket*) They brought him to the bus in these.

KING

(*A bit taken aback by handcuffs*)
I'll make a note of it.

IRVIN

I think he ought to be given disciplinary action. He took a swing at—one of the men. Even knocked him out. He jumped this man from behind and knocked him out.

KING

In the barracks here?

IRVIN

Back at the bus.

KING
*(Pause)*
I'll make a note of it.

IRVIN
I thought he ought to be reported to the Squadron Com-
mander, that's what. (KING *freezes for a moment*) I mean, I
think it's my duty to see that he—

KING
Any reporting is done around here, *I* do it.

IRVIN
Sure you do, and this fellow Stockdale is a real troublemaker and he—

KING
*(Sitting on bed)*
Sonny, look; how long have you been in the service?

IRVIN
About six hours, I guess. I had R.O.T.C., though.

KING
Uh-huh . . . And they told you it was all efficiency and
getting things done and standing at attention and running
around? (*Taking off shoes*) I been in for eighteen years, and
it ain't like you think at all. It's a quiet, peaceful life . . . if
everybody minds their own business. It's like there's a big
lake, nice and calm; I'm in one canoe, you're in another, the
Captain's in a canoe, the Colonel . . . You know what you
do when you complain to somebody, or report somebody, or

27

request something? (IRVIN *shakes his head*) You make waves. (*Puts his feet into big woolly slippers, rises, goes to table, takes cup and saucer from shelf, pours coffee. IRVIN, meanwhile, puts handcuffs on forms and goes to door.*)

#### IRVIN

Well, I thought the Captain would want to know, if he's got a troublemaker in the outfit.

#### KING

Look, Sonny, I hate to pull rank, but for your information, you got the smallest canoe in the whole damn lake! Good afternoon, Private.

(IRVIN *exits, closing door.* KING *stretches out on his bunk.*)

#### RADIO ANNOUNCER

Our next request comes from Master Sergeant Orville C. King at the Air Force Classification Center. Here you are, Sergeant.

(KING *beams. The radio plays "Flow Gently, Sweet Afton,"* KING *sips his coffee thoughtfully, and the lights slowly fade.*)

(*Lights come up on a double-decker bunk.* BEN, *in underwear, manages to climb on to upper bunk, with* WILL's *assistance.*)

#### BEN

Don't boost—I can make it.

#### WILL

Ben, I wish you would take the bottom one.

BEN

No, sir. Just hand me my bag.

WILL

(*Doing so*)

Honest, I like sleeping high.

BEN

No, sir. You sat on the bottom bunk first.

WILL

I didn't mean nothin' by it. Honest I didn't.

BEN

First come, first served. That's the military way.

VOICE

(*Off*)

Lights out in five minutes.

WILL

(*Pulling on* BEN's *bag*)

C'mon, Ben.

BEN

I won't, I tell you!
(IRVIN *and two* INDUCTEES *enter from right.*)

IRVIN

Let that man alone, Stockdale! Get your hands off that
man's things! (WILL, *wide-eyed, withdraws his hand.* BEN

29

*falls back on bunk*) They brought you to the bus in handcuffs and I'm beginning to think I never should've taken 'em off you!

WILL

Irvin, I wasn't doin' anythin'. I was just—

IRVIN

I've stood about as much as I'm *gonna* stand out of you! One lucky punch don't make no champion. If you want to start some more fighting go after somebody your own size, not some skinny little—

BEN

(*Swinging his feet off top bunk*)

You watch your mouth! Why don't you mind your own business anyhow?

IRVIN

Look, this fellow was going to—

BEN

That's between him and me! Nobody asked you to butt in!

WILL

Now, Ben, don't . . .

IRVIN

I was only trying to do you a favor, Junior!

BEN

Who you calling Junior? Who asked you anything any-how?

IRVIN

All right. If that's the way you feel about it, all right. You want to be buddies with the draft-dodger, *be* buddies with the draft-dodger. Go ahead . . .

BEN

That's the way I feel about it.

IRVIN

(*Backing away*)
You better just get into bed and *don't start no trouble in this barracks!* Get into bed!

WILL

I was just goin' to, Irvin.

FIRST INDUCTEE

Give him time, Irvin. Beds is strange to Plowboy; he's used to sleepin' with the hogs!
(INDUCTEES *laugh*, WILL *joins in*, BEN *glares*. IRVIN *and* INDUCTEES, *laughing, move off*.)

BEN

(*Livid*)
What's the matter with you anyhow?

WILL

Me?

BEN

Taking their insults all day and hee-hawing like a danged donkey!

31

WILL

Ah, they don't mean nothin', Ben. And besides, that one about sleepin' with the hogs was kind of funny.

(*Starts taking off pants.*)

BEN

(*Getting under blankets*)

Aw . . .

WILL

I figger if we just laugh with 'em, Ben, pretty soon they'll get tired of carryin' on, and that way there won't be no ruckus or nothin'.

BEN

You think laughing is gonna stop these guys? A good licking is all they understand!

WILL

(*Hangs pants on end of bunk*)

You think so?

BEN

I know so! . . . And you hee-hawing like a danged donkey!

(*He turns over, putting his back to* WILL. WILL *scratches his head, sits on bottom bunk. Lights dim down and a bugle starts playing "Taps."* WILL *listens for a moment.*)

WILL

(*To audience*)

Somebody brung their trumpet.

(THIRD INDUCTEE *crosses.*)

FIRST INDUCTEE

Lonesome for the hogs, Plowboy?
(WILL *laughs half-heartedly.*)


WILL

(*To audience*)

I reckon Ben knew what he was talkin' about when he said laughin' warn't gonna do no good. But I figgered I couldn't start bangin' away at 'em with no reason so I set around waitin' for someone to give me a reason.


FOURTH INDUCTEE

(*Passing* WILL)

Ain't used to sleeping indoors, are you, Plowboy?


WILL

(*To audience*)

I didn't feel as how that was quite enough.
(IRVIN *and his two sidekicks return.*)


IRVIN

Get in bed, Plowboy.


WILL

(*To audience*)

That warn't enough.


IRVIN

(*To* WILL)

That is, if you can lift those big clumsy feet of yours.

WILL

(*To audience*)
That warn't enough either.

IRVIN

(*To* BEN)
Don't wet the bed, Junior, or Mama will spank.

WILL

(*To audience*)
That were. (*He slugs* IRVIN *and* IRVIN *goes down*) No stayin'
power at all. (*Other* INDUCTEES *attack.* BEN *hops onto one's
shoulders and pummels his head.* WILL *dispatches the others
with great ease, punctuating the action with the following
lines*) No more muscle than a rabbit . . . Livin' in town,
that's what does it . . . They stay up till close on to ten
o'clock every night! Eat all them fancy foods . . . Orange
juice. . . . Won't touch green peas unless the shells is off 'em!
Surprises me they got what little strength they have . . .
(*All the assailants are floored by now. They stagger away.*
WILL *comes downstage, brushing off his hands*) But there was
a whole lot of 'em, so it was a pretty good fight anyhow!
(*Turning up to* BEN) Warn't it, Ben?

BEN

Aww . . .

WILL

Could've been better, but it wasn't bad.

BEN

Dog it, Will. This will mess up everything!

34

**WILL**

What will, Ben?

**BEN**

Fighting—in the barracks.

**WILL**

But you said a lickin' was all they'd understand.

**BEN**

Not in the barracks! One of them's bound to talk about it. Dog it, I'll never get into the Infantry now . . . starting a big ruckus . . . I figgered if we kept our mouths shut and didn't do nothin to nobody we might get transferred—but now—

**WILL**

Both of us?

**BEN**

But now they're sure to talk about the fight—they're bound to!

**WILL**

No they won't, Ben. If one of them says anythin', I'll take him out back and whomp him good.

**BEN**

Now there you go again, Will! You think they want folks in the Infantry that acts like that? No sir, they want folks who can take it and keep their mouths shut, the way a man ought to do. Transfer? We'll be lucky if they don't transfer us into the Navy—walking around in them li'l ole white uniforms!

35

WILL

You want both of us to transfer, Ben?


BEN

Don't you understand, Will? It's the Infantry does the real fighting . . . the rest is just helpers. Look at The War Between The States. How about that?


WILL

Yeh! How about that!


BEN

· See what I mean? Listen, every man in my whole family's been in the Infantry, clear back to Great-Grandpa! You know what he done? Fought with Stonewall Jackson at Chancellorsville, that's what!


WILL

Licked him good too, I bet!


BEN

By dog, first thing tomorrow morning I'm going to get the Sergeant's permission to see the Captain. I'll give him Ma's letter . . . (*Takes letter from under pillow, looks at it*) Aww . . . (*Throws letter disgustedly on floor*) What's the use! (*Climbs into bunk and under blankets.*)


WILL

But, Ben, maybe you'll get to like the Air Force. Zoomin' all over the sky, shoutin' Roger and Wilco and everythin'. Maybe it won't be so bad.

BEN

Bad! You know what they call men in the Air Force? Airmen! Like something out of a danged funny book! How you gonna like it when somebody calls you Airman?

WILL

By God, I just don't think I'd stand for it.

BEN

AIRMAN!
(*He buries his head in the pillow.*)

WILL

Ben! (*No response*) Hey, Ben! (*Still no reply.* WILL *picks up the letter which* BEN *has discarded. He looks at the envelope*) By dog!

(*Lights fade, leaving only a pin-spot on* WILL *as he takes trousers from bunk, pulls them on, tiptoes down to door of* KING's *room and knocks lightly. He buttons trousers and knocks again, harder. He fastens belt and knocks once more, a real rafter-shaker. There is an excited bumping and fumbling from* KING's *room.*)

KING

All right! I'm up! I'm up! All right! (*More bumping and fumbling. Lights come up;* KING's *table lamp. He almost knocks it over. One leg is in his trousers, one arm in his shirt.* WILL *enters room*) All right! I'm up!

WILL

Howdy! I'm Will Stockdale.

37

KING

(*Struggling into uniform*)

I didn't hear no whistle. Tell the men to line up in back. If the Captain comes around tell him I'm checking on who overslept. I'll be out as soon as I . . . (*Looks at* WILL, *looks around, looks at wrist watch*) It's ten o'clock . . . at night.

WILL

It is? (KING *shoves his wrist watch under* WILL's *nose*) Ooh! That's the prettiest watch . . .

KING

(*Dazed by the enormity of the sin*)

You woke me.

WILL

You said to knock before enterin'.

KING

(*Sinking on bunk, removing uniform*)

Why did you wake me?

WILL

Well, this ain't nothin' personal against you, Sergeant, or that we don't like your barracks or nothin' like that. What it is is Ben's got these six brothers that are all Infantry—that's my new buddy Ben that's sleepin' out there—so naturally he don't want to be in the Air Force, I mean with the Infantry doin' the real fightin' and the Air Force just bein' the helpers. You know, like in The War Between The States. So he wants to transfer to the Infantry and he asked me to go along with him. I figgered you could do it for us. I heared what you said out there, about how you was here to help us durin' these first difficult days of military service.

KING

(*Stares, turns away*)
Why do they send all the bums and idiots to my barracks?

WILL

They do?

KING

(*Turning to him again*)
Yes. Yes, they do.

WILL

Sho' must be a mess.

KING

(*Rising*)
Now look, whatever-your-name-is, I want you to get—

WILL

Stockdale.

KING

Stockdale. I want you to get out of this room and—Stock-dale . . . (*Turns to table, lifts handcuffs*) Stockdale . . . (*Turning to* WILL *again*) Now don't start anything with me, you hear. Just get out of here and go to sleep, that's all.

WILL

Yes, sir. (*As he exits*) Ben *did* say the Captain was the one to see.

KING

STOCKDALE! (*Rushes after him*) Where are you going?

WILL

To the Captain.

KING

No . . . no . . . You can't . . .
(*Pushes* WILL *back into room.*)

WILL

Ben knows all about doin' things military-like, and he said
the Captain was—

KING

Stockdale, you're . . . you're . . . (*Makes wave-making
gesture*) You can't *do* this. This Captain'll rip off your stripes
as soon as look at you.

WILL

I ain't got no stripes.

KING

You'll never get transfers waking him up. He won't understand; believe me, he won't!

WILL

I'll go over it real slow.

KING

Oh Lord . . . Look, this Captain . . . he . . . he won't
do a favor for anybody unless they do a favor for him first!
That's it. Now how would you like to do a big favor for the
Captain?

WILL

Me?

KING

Come on. (*Virtually drags* WILL *across stage*) You do one for him, he'll do one for me, and I do one for you. That's the way it works in the service.

(*Lights come up in latrine and fade out in* KING'S *room.*)

KING

Do you know what this is, Stockdale?

WILL

Well, it's kind of a big outhouse, ain't it?

KING

We call it the latrine.

WILL

(*Looking around*)
La-trine . . . How about that . . .

KING

You might say it's the Captain's hobby. He inspects it every chance he gets, and when everything is sparkling, the Captain sparkles too. (*Takes long-handled brush from wall and gives it to* WILL) You stay in here and get things all cleaned up. You are the Officer in Charge.

WILL

(*Overwhelmed*)

In charge?

41

KING

Every last one! All yours!


WILL

Golly!


KING

(*Going to door*)
Now stay in here, you understand? Don't go no place.


WILL

You bet! Good night!


KING

(*Incredulously*)
Good night . . .
(*Exits, shaking head wonderingly.*)


WILL

(*Calling after him*)
Say, thanks! (*He tucks handle of brush under his belt and begins collecting trash from floor. Door of* KING'S *room is heard slamming. To audience*) Well! It just goes to show you how good things happen to you when you least expect 'em. (*Hums at his work*) I stayed Officer in Charge of this here la-trine all night, a'rubbin' and a'scrubbin' and doin' my best to make things sparkle like Sergeant King said. (*Puts trash in can*) And by the time mornin' come—if you'll excuse my braggin'—I think I done a right good job of it. Sergeant King was real pleased with how things come out.
(KING *enters latrine.*)

42

KING

Beautiful! Beautiful . . . beautiful . . . (*At commodes*)
. . . beau—ti—ful!

WILL

Shucks, it ain't hard . . .

KING

(*Looks around incredulously*)
Wait till the *Captain* sees this! He inspects this place like it
was an operating room where they was getting ready to *cut
out his heart!* Never in your life have you seen such a man
for sticking his head *right down into* things!

WILL

You figger he'll like what I done?

KING

He'll be a new man. . . . (KING *stares some more, then
goes to* WILL *and puts his hand solemnly on his shoulder*)
Will . . . How would you like to be . . . Permanent Latrine Orderly?

WILL

Permanent Latrine Orderly . . .

KING

P.L.O.!

WILL

Golly . . .

KING

You'll keep this place all the time like it is now, the Captain'll get off my back . . .

WILL

Gee, I sure would like to do it, Sergeant. Only I was set on helpin' Ben get those transfers. He's my buddy.

KING

Ain't I your buddy?

WILL

You are?

KING

You help me, I'll help Ben. But don't say a word about this outside of this room, you understand? I'm going straight over to the Record Section and fix it with some friends of mine.

WILL

Don't I have to go get them tests you talked about yesterday, to get myself classified?

KING

(At door)
No, Will . . . (A *final enraptured look at latrine*) . . . you've *been* classified.
(*He exits.* WILL *turns happily to audience.*)

WILL

Well, didn't *that* make me feel pretty good? (*Hangs brush on wall, takes tie and khaki shirt from hook, puts them on during following*) I worked just as hard as I could all week long. Of course, every time I seen Ben, he took on right fierce about how it was against the rules for me to be permanent in the latrine. He didn't mean nothin' by it, though. Anyhow I worked real hard; I scrubbed what was for scrubbin' and polished what was for polishin', and what was left over, I painted. And by Saturday, when the Captain come to inspect, I had everythin' so white and shiny you couldn't hardly look at it without squenchin' up your eyes. Them faucets for instance; I polished them so hard they don't say hot and cold no more!

(*Smoothes down his hair and comes to attention facing the door. Door flies open.*)

### KING

Ten-hut!

(KING *holds door for* CAPTAIN, *then follows him in.*)

### WILL

(*Saluting*)

Latrine ready for inspection, sir!

(CAPTAIN *returns salute, sees glittering latrine, lowers arm slowly.* WILL *drops salute.* CAPTAIN, *wide-eyed, turns to* KING. KING *smiles complacently.* CAPTAIN *moves incredulously about latrine.*)

### CAPTAIN

This is incredible . . . This is absolutely . . . incredible! I'm pleased! No, no . . . no, I'm *happy!*

### KING

Thank you, sir, thank you.

CAPTAIN

(*Inspects commodes, thoroughly, then beams at* WILL)
You the one on latrine duty today, Private?

WILL

Yes, sir. All week, sir.
(KING *clears his throat forebodingly.*)

CAPTAIN

Well, you are to be congratulated. (*Examines sink*) Just
look at the—(*Turns to* WILL) What did you say?

WILL

Me? Nothin', sir.

CAPTAIN

Something about all week.

WILL

Well, I done my best in one day, but to be fair with you it
took a week of rubbin' and scrubbin' to get it like this.

CAPTAIN

(*To* KING)
Is this man being punished for—

WILL

Heck no, sir! I'm P.L.O.!

CAPTAIN

What?

WILL

Permanent Latrine Orderly.

KING

Stockdale . . .

WILL

Don't credit me none, sir. It's *all* Sergeant King's doin'. He's even got it fixed up so's I don't have to get classified!

KING

Sir—

CAPTAIN

That's . . . that's impossible!

WILL

Oh no, sir. He fixed it with some friends of his.

KING

Stockdale . . .

WILL

It was him got me to work so hard, tellin' me how latrines is your hobby and stickin' your head into things and all.

KING

Sir, I can . . .

WILL

Now don't be bashful, Sergeant! Sir, I been wantin' to tell you what a good sergeant he is. He solves our problems for us, and he helps us out on our difficult days of military service, and I reckon he's just about the best danged sergeant there is in the whole danged Air Force! (*Pause*) Sir, you really ought to get up off'n his back.

(CAPTAIN *turns slowly to* KING; KING *turns slowly to liquid.*)

CAPTAIN

How long have you been a sergeant? (KING *gives an incomprehensible mumble*) Speak up!

KING

Sixteen years, sir.

CAPTAIN

How long do you expect to remain a sergeant?

KING

(*Hopefully*)

Twelve years?

CAPTAIN

You will remain a sergeant for exactly one week. One week! Unless this man completes the entire classification process and is shipped out with the group he came in with. Do you understand? Unless this man is out of here by the end of next week, you will not be in charge of this barracks, you will not be a sergeant; you will in all probability be a permanent latrine orderly. P.L.O.!

KING

(*Saluting weakly*)

Yes, sir!

(CAPTAIN *returns salute and goes to door. Stops outside latrine doorway, turns and speaks to* WILL.)

48

CAPTAIN

This is not your fault, Private. You've done a fine job. This is the cleanest latrine I've seen in my entire career.

WILL

Thank you, sir. My aim was to get it just as clean as that operatin' room where they're gettin' ready to cut out your heart. (*Before* WILL *has finished the above,* KING *has leaped across room and slammed door in* CAPTAIN'S *face. He remains against door, staring at* WILL, *trembling*) You forgot to ask him about the transfers.

KING

What happened? What did you do it for?

WILL

Well, I couldn't see no sense in *me* gettin' all the credit.

KING

(*Coming close to* WILL, *not daring to touch him*)
Look, Will, we got to get you classified. We got to get you out of here . . .

WILL

(*Pause*)
You don't want me around no more? I thought we was buddies.

KING

(*Quickly*)
It ain't what I want, Will; it's what the Captain wants. (*Leading* WILL *out of latrine*) Come on, we gotta get you classified in a hurry. There's all kinds of tests you'll have to take,

**49**

and people you'll have to talk with. You'll have to work real hard.

> (KING *and* WILL *are now spotlighted downstage, as rest of stage fades into darkness.*)

### WILL

I'll work hard, all right, but I don't know . . . The last time I took a test was close on to five years ago, and then it was just one of them tests where you try this fellow's toothpaste for ten days and see if'n your teeth don't get brighter. (*Pause*) I failed.

### KING

> (*Looks desperate. He shows* WILL *his wrist watch*)
Look, you been admiring this watch of mine, haven't you?

### WILL

I sure have! It's the prettiest . . .

### KING

If you're ready to ship out by next Saturday like the Captain said—it's yours!

### WILL

Mine?

### KING

Yours!

### WILL

Gol-ly!

### KING

So you're going to try your hardest, right?

WILL

Right!

KING

And not waste no time?

WILL

No sir!

KING

Good! Good boy! Now first thing Monday morning we start Classification. You just stay right here and relax, rest your head. I'm going over to the testing area and see if I can . . . uh, borrow some of the tests.

(*He vanishes into the darkness.* WILL *turns to audience.*)

WILL

That Classification was really somethin'. They got this great big buildin' all full of doctors and nurses and officers— all of 'em walkin' around real quickety-quick and not smilin' at nobody. And first thing you knowed, one of 'em was mashin' down your tongue with an ice cream stick! You think I'm makin' this up. It's the truth! One of them fellows was even goin' around poppin' everybody in the knee with a little rubber hammer!

(*Lights fade up on a hallway with three doors marked "Manual Dexterity," "Psychiatrist" and "Oculist."* OF-FICERS, INDUCTEES, NURSES *and* DOCTORS *cross back and forth. Typewriters and tabulators can be heard.* WILL *sets about rolling a cigarette.*)

FIRST CORPORAL

(*Crossing*)

Hey, you there! (WILL *turns*) No smoking! (*Points to wall sign*) Don't you know how to read?

WILL

(*To audience*)

Good thing Pa ain't around to hear that. Well, anyhow, I did pretty good on it all. The written tests was exactly the same as the ones Sergeant King borrowed, but the only trouble was the Sergeant spent so much time drummin' the answers into me, there was hardly no time left to study the questions they joined up with. So in the tests, the answers was easy, but the questions was real hard. By Friday afternoon, I was down to the last three tests, and Sergeant King said it looked like maybe I might get myself classified for Gunnery School.

(*"Manual Dexterity" door opens.* KING *sticks his head out.*)

KING

Will! Come on! (WILL *goes up to* KING) Corporal's waiting for you.

(*Lights come up in "Manual Dexterity" room and fade out in hallway. An officious little* CORPORAL *stands waiting; a large irregularly shaped link in each hand.*)

SECOND CORPORAL

(*Motions* WILL *into chair*)

What we do here, Private, is evaluate your manual dexterity. On a time scale in relation to digital-visual co-ordination.

(*He holds up links*) Two irregular steel links . . . (*He fits them together, a complex job*) . . . which can be interconnected . . . thusly. (*Holds them up, joined, then separates them*) I separate them . . . (*Joins them again*) . . . I join them. It will be your task, Private, when I give the signal, to place the two links in the interconnected relationship I have just demonstrated.

> (*He puts a link in each of* WILL's *hands.* WILL *looks at them confusedly.*)

#### WILL

I put 'em together?

#### SECOND CORPORAL

That's right, you "put them together." I'll time you. Three minutes is passing.

> (*Winds stop watch.*)

#### KING

Whatever you do, don't get nervous.

#### SECOND CORPORAL

Ready? (*Raises watch*) Go!

> (WILL *slowly touches one link against the other, baffled.* KING *is on top of him.*)

#### KING

There we go! At-a-boy! Put 'em together!

#### SECOND CORPORAL

Sergeant! Please. No one ever does it in less than two minutes! Please! You're not even supposed to be in here!

> (*He pulls* KING *away. They move aside, conversing in low tones.*)

53

KING

No, no. It's okay. You see, I'm rushing him through so he can catch up with the group he came in with. He's a special case.

SECOND CORPORAL

Well, I'll have to ask you not to speak to him during the actual testing. It's a difficult problem and requires his full attention.

(*As* KING *and* SECOND CORPORAL *continue their exchange,* WILL *is busily wrenching open one link, shoving it through its mate and compressing the pair into something resembling a bowknot.*)

WILL

I'm done.

KING

Stop the watch!

SECOND CORPORAL

Done? (*Looking at watch*) In fourteen seconds? (*Takes links from* WILL) He . . . look what he . . . look! (*Tries to separate links.*)

KING

He put them together, didn't he?

SECOND CORPORAL

(*Running into hallway.* KING *and* WILL *follow. Lights dim out in room and come up in hallway*) Corporal!

**KING**

Now what are you making a fuss about? You said put 'em together and he—

**SECOND CORPORAL**

(*To* FIRST CORPORAL *as he enters*)
Look! Look what he's done, for Pete's sake. How you supposed to mark him on that?

**FIRST CORPORAL**

You're supposed to be grading this. Can't you do a simple thing like that?
(*Exits.*)

**SECOND CORPORAL**

(*Calling after him*)
I'm supposed to mark it down if they put it back together or not and there ain't supposed to be but one way of doing it, and he sure didn't do it that way. . . . How you gonna mark a thing like that? And who's gonna pay for these things? (*To* WILL) Sixteen dollars they cost. If you think I'm gonna pay sixteen lousy dollars . . .

**KING**

(*Advancing on him, soothingly*)
Corporal, Corporal . . .

**SECOND CORPORAL**

Sixteen lousy dollars!

**KING**

Corporal . . . I'll be *glad* to pay the sixteen lousy dollars.

SECOND CORPORAL

You will?

KING

Sure. If he passed the test . . .

SECOND CORPORAL

But he did it completely wrong. He was supposed to—

KING

(*Taking* CORPORAL's *arm and leading him off*)
Now let's take this logically; you need some money and I
need for him to pass the test. . . .
        (WILL *watches them go. Door of* PSYCHIATRIST's *office*
        *opens and* BEN *emerges.*)

BEN

(*Seeing* WILL)

Will!

WILL

(*Turning*)

Ben!
        (*They rush to each other and pump hands.*)

BEN

I ain't hardly seen you all day! What you been doing, clas-
sifying?

WILL

Yeah!

BEN

Find out where you're going?

56

**WILL**

Sergeant King says if I pass the eye test I'll be goin' to Gunnery School!

**BEN**

That's where I'm going if I pass the eye test!

**WILL**

How about that—
(*Flips* BEN's *tie out of his shirt.*)

**BEN**

(*Suddenly deflated*)
Yeah. How about that.

**WILL**

Ben, you ain't *still* sad about not bein' in the Infantry?

**BEN**

The Captain never even read my letter. I even asked that there psychiatrist.

**WILL**

What did he say?

**BEN**

He didn't say nothing. I don't think he understands so good. Looks like I'm stuck with the Air Force.

**WILL**

But Ben, maybe it's really the Air Force that's the real soldiers and the Infantry that's just the helpers.

57

BEN

Never.

WILL

What about that movie they showed us, about that airplane that goes up *fifty* thousand feet, and makes the blood boil up inside you and kills you in ten seconds! It's the Air Age, Ben! And the gunner is right up there with the pilot and the bombardier and all the others!

BEN

Yeah! Bombardier! Throws bombs! But who does he throw 'em at? The infantry, that's who!

WILL

And medals! Ooh, the way that fellow took on! You get one for practically everythin' in the Air Force. They even give you one for just bein' there and not doin' nothin' wrong. How about that!

BEN

Wait till my brothers find out. Airman!
(BEN *pulls his cap from his belt and hurls it to the floor. As he does so, a Negro* LIEUTENANT *is passing by. He stops.*)

LIEUTENANT

Private!

BEN

(*Snapping to attention*)

Sir!

LIEUTENANT

That's no way to treat government property.

**BEN**

Yes, sir!

**LIEUTENANT**

Pick up your cap, Private.

**BEN**

Yes, sir.
(*Stoops to retrieve cap.*)

**LIEUTENANT**

You shouldn't be loitering here anyhow.

**BEN**

(*Rising quickly and coming to attention again*)
We're being classified, sir.

**LIEUTENANT**

(*To* WILL)
I'm looking for Sergeant King. Do you know him?

**WILL**

(*Gaping*)
Sure do . . . He's ourn . . .

**LIEUTENANT**

Where is he?

**WILL**

He went down there with a corporal in tow. He's havin'
trouble gettin' me classified.

**LIEUTENANT**

*(Knowingly)*

Uh-huh. *(Starting to go)* Pick up that cap, Private.

**BEN**

*(Retrieves cap)*

Yes, sir.

**LIEUTENANT**

And let's get that tie tucked in.
*(Exits.)*

**BEN**

Yes, sir. *(To* WILL*)* What's the matter with you? Don't you know enough to stand at attention and salute an officer?

**WILL**

*(Still gaping after the* LIEUTENANT*)*

You know, he talked whiter than I do.

**BEN**

Whiter than you do? Listen, he was an officer, that's all!

**WILL**

And I'll bet he's a good one, too, so snappy and all . . . *(Pause)* I'm homesick . . .

**BEN**

Will, when a man's in uniform, he ain't black or white or yellow or nothing! You ain't supposed to notice the color of a man in uniform!

**WILL**

You ain't?

**BEN**

No sir!

**WILL**

Ben, you mean . . . when that Lieutenant come over . . .
you didn't notice he was . . . is it all right if I say colored?

**BEN**

All I saw was a lieutenant, period!

**WILL**

A colored lieutenant.

**BEN**

A lieutenant! Can't you understand nothing, Will? The
only thing that's important in the service is rank! If a man's
an officer, he's higher than you, even if he's green with purple
spots!

**WILL**

Oh, now, Ben . . .

**BEN**

Rank! That's all! A man in uniform don't see nothing else!

**WILL**

Well, dang it, Ben . . . I'm a man in uniform all right
and the minute he come in here I seen his face was darker
than ourn!

**BEN**

Honest, Will. Sometimes I wonder how come they ever
took you in the draft at all!

(KING *and* SECOND CORPORAL *re-enter, both smiling,* KING *pocketing his wallet.* SECOND CORPORAL *exits into "Manual Dexterity" room.*)

KING

Well, it looks like we're just liable to get you classified after all. It goes to show what the Air Force has come down to.

THIRD CORPORAL

(*Entering from* PSYCHIATRIST's *office with form in hand. To* KING)
Is this fellow Whitledge in your group?

BEN

That's me, Corporal.

KING

Yeah—that's him.

THIRD CORPORAL

Psychiatrist says he has a secondary anxiety with inferiority and systematized delusions of persecution.

KING

I ain't surprised.

THIRD CORPORAL

Recommends he be considered for transfer to the Infantry.

BEN

The *Infantry!*

THIRD CORPORAL

Don't get excited. He didn't say you have to.

WILL

That's what Ben's always wantin', Corporal.

BEN

Just what do I have to do?

THIRD CORPORAL
(*Gives* BEN *a form*)
Here—fill this out. (*To* KING) Soon as he's finished, buck
it through to the Colonel for approval.

KING

Okay. If that's what the crazy kid wants.

WILL

How about that, Ben—you made it!

BEN

Just wait till I tell my brothers!

THIRD CORPORAL
(*Holding out another form*)
Okay, Stockdale—Psychiatrist.

KING

(*Takes form from* CORPORAL, *who exits*)
Oh Lord. Now Will, listen carefully. The psychiatrist test
is one I couldn't get the questions for because there ain't any.

63

The doctor just asks you whatever pops into his head. So keep your wits about you.

WILL

I'll try. Maybe I can get a transfer too, huh, Ben?

KING

He'll just ask you stuff like "What do you dream?"

WILL

Okay. (*Touches* BEN) Maybe he'll give me a transfer too, huh, Ben?

BEN

Yeah, sure . . .

KING

Safest thing, I guess, is to say you never dream at all.

WILL

See you later, Ben.
    (*Exits into* PSYCHIATRIST'S *office.*)

KING

No dreams! Oh, jeez . . .
    (*Begins pacing.*)

BEN

Do you think he can?

KING

Can what?

BEN

Get transferred too? Maybe you could talk to the doctor.

KING

Listen! Don't you complicate things.

BEN

I just wish Will was going too. I mean it'd be more fun . . .

KING

Listen, Whitledge, you take care of yourself. *I'll* take care
of *him.*

BEN

Okay, okay . . .
    (BEN *begins filling out his form as the lights fade out in*
    *hallway and fade up in* PSYCHIATRIST'S *office.* PSYCHI-
    ATRIST, *a major, signs and stamps a paper before him,*
    *then takes form from* WILL, *seated next to desk.* PSY-
    CHIATRIST *looks at form, looks at* WILL. *A moment of*
    *silence.)*

WILL

I never have no dreams at all.

PSYCHIATRIST

    (*A pause. He looks carefully at* WILL, *looks at form*)
Where you from, Stockdale?

WILL

Georgia.

PSYCHIATRIST

That's . . . not much of a state, is it?

65

**WILL**

Well . . . I don't live all over the state. I just live in this one little place in it.

**PSYCHIATRIST**

That's where "Tobacco Road" is, Georgia.

**WILL**

Not around my section. (*Pause*) Maybe you're from a different part than me?

**PSYCHIATRIST**

I've never been there. What's more I don't think I would ever *want to* go there. What's your reaction to that?

**WILL**

Well, I don't know.

**PSYCHIATRIST**

I think I would sooner live in the rottenest pigsty in Alabama or Tennessee than in the fanciest mansion in all of Georgia. What about that?

**WILL**

Well, sir, I think where you want to live is your business.

**PSYCHIATRIST**

(*Pause, staring*)

You don't mind if someone says something bad about Georgia?

**WILL**

I ain't heared nobody say nothin' bad about Georgia.

PSYCHIATRIST

What do you think I've been saying?

WILL

Well, to tell you the truth, I ain't been able to get too much sense out of it. Don't you know?

PSYCHIATRIST

Watch your step, young man. (*Pause*) We psychiatrists call this attitude of yours "resistance."

WILL

You do?

PSYCHIATRIST

You sense that this interview is a threat to your security. You feel yourself in danger.

WILL

Well, kind of I do. If'n I don't get classified Sergeant King won't give me the wrist watch. (PSYCHIATRIST *stares at* WILL *uncomprehendingly*) He *won't*! He said I only gets it if I'm classified inside a week.

PSYCHIATRIST

(*Turns forlornly to papers on desk. A bit subdued*)
You get along all right with your mother?

WILL

No, sir, I can't hardly say that I do—

PSYCHIATRIST

(*Cutting in*)

She's very strict? Always hovering over you?

WILL

No, sir, just the opposite—

PSYCHIATRIST

She's never there.

WILL

That's right.

PSYCHIATRIST

You resent this neglect, don't you?

WILL

No, I don't resent nothin'.

PSYCHIATRIST

(*Leaning forward paternally*)

There's nothing to be ashamed of, son. It's a common situation. Does she ever beat you?

WILL

No!

PSYCHIATRIST

(*Silkily*)

So defensive. It's not easy to talk about your mother, is it.

WILL

No, sir. She died when I was borned.

PSYCHIATRIST

*(A long, sick pause)*
You . . . could have told me that sooner . . .


WILL

*(Looks hang-dog.* PSYCHIATRIST *returns to papers.* WILL *glances up at him)*
Do you hate *your* Mama? (PSYCHIATRIST's *head snaps up, glaring)* I figgered as how you said it was so common . . .


PSYCHIATRIST

I do not hate my mother.


WILL

I should hope not! *(Pause)* What does she beat you or somethin'?


PSYCHIATRIST

*(Glares again, drums his fingers briefly on table. Steeling himself, more to self than* WILL*)*
This is a transference. You're taking all your stored up antagonisms and loosing them in my direction. Transference. It happens every day. . . .


WILL

*(Excited)*
It does? To the Infantry?


PSYCHIATRIST

*(Aghast)*
The Infantry?

**WILL**

You give Ben a transfer. I wish you'd give me one too. I'd sure love to go along with him.

**PSYCHIATRIST**

Stop! (*The pause is a long one this time. Finally* PSYCHIA-TRIST *points at papers*) There are a few more topics we have to cover. We will not talk about transfers, we will not talk about my mother. We will only talk about what *I* want to talk about, do you understand?

**WILL**

Yes, sir.

**PSYCHIATRIST**

Now then—your father. (*Quickly*) Living?

**WILL**

Yes, sir.

**PSYCHIATRIST**

Do you get along with him okay?

**WILL**

Yes, sir.

**PSYCHIATRIST**

Does he ever beat you?

**WILL**

You bet!

**PSYCHIATRIST**

Hard?

70

WILL

And how! Boy, there ain't nobody can beat like my Pa can!

PSYCHIATRIST

(*Beaming*)

So *this* is where the antagonism comes from! (*Pause*) You hate your father, don't you.

WILL

No . . . I got an uncle I hate! Every time he comes out to the house he's always wantin' to rassle with the mule, and the mule gets all wore out, and *he* gets all wore out . . . Well, I don't really *hate* him; I just ain't exactly partial to him.

PSYCHIATRIST

(*Pause*)

Did I ask you about your uncle?

WILL

I thought you wanted to talk about hatin' people.

PSYCHIATRIST

(*Glares, drums his fingers, retreats to form. Barely audible*)

Now—girls. How do you like girls?

WILL

What girls is that, sir?

PSYCHIATRIST

Just girls. Just any girls.

71

WILL

Well, I don't like just any girls. There's one old girl back home that ain't got hair no longer than a hound-dog's and she's always—

PSYCHIATRIST

No! Look, when I say girls I don't mean any one specific girl. I mean girls in general; women, sex! Didn't that father of yours ever sit down and have a talk with you?

WILL

Sure he did.

PSYCHIATRIST

Well?

WILL

Well what?

PSYCHIATRIST

What did he say?

WILL

(*With a snicker*)

Well, there was this one about these two travelin' salesmen that their car breaks down in the middle of this terrible storm—

PSYCHIATRIST

Stop!

WILL

—so they stop at this farmhouse where the farmer has fourteen daughters who was—

**PSYCHIATRIST**

*Stop!*

**WILL**

You heared it already?

**PSYCHIATRIST**

(*Writing furiously on form*)
No, I did not hear it already . . .

**WILL**

Well, what did you stop me for? It's a real knee-slapper.
You see, the fourteen daughters is all studyin' to be trombone
players and—

**PSYCHIATRIST**

(*Shoving form at* WILL)
Here. Go. Good-bye. You're through. You're normal. Good-
bye. Go. Go.

**WILL**

(*Takes form and stands, a bit confused by it all*)
Sir, if girls is what you want to talk about, you ought to
come down to the barracks some night. The younger fellows
there is always tellin' spicy stories and all like that.

(*Lights fade out in* PSYCHIATRIST's *office and come up
in hallway.* KING *and* BEN *are as before.* IRVIN *emerges
from oculist's office, putting on his dark glasses.* BEN
*exits into oculist's office.*)

**KING**

Irvin! How's the eye test?

IRVIN

A snap.

KING

Listen, I want you to coach Stockdale. He's going in there next.

IRVIN

Now, listen, Sarge . . .

KING

You'll coach him!
(*Door of* PSYCHIATRIST'S *office opens and* WILL *emerges.*)

WILL

(*Over his shoulder*)
Excuse me for sayin' it, sir, but I don't think a fellow your age would be so confused about it all if you went out and *seen* some girls once in a while.
(*Closes door.*)

KING

(*Seizing him*)
What are you doing? Are you crazy?

WILL

That fellow's in pretty bad shape, Sergeant.
(*Handing* KING *his form.*)

KING

(*Looking at form*)
What did he say? (BEN *comes out of oculist's office*) Thank the Lord! Good boy! Normal!

74

WILL

Hey, Ben. You fill out that transfer yet?

BEN

It's only an application, Will. Don't mean a thing unless the Colonel okays it.
(*Hands application form to* KING.)

WILL

I asked that fellow in there to give me a transfer too, but all he done was squench up his eyes.
(*The Negro* LIEUTENANT *enters.*)

LIEUTENANT

Sergeant, is your group all through?

KING

Just these two to go and that's the lot.

LIEUTENANT
(*Consulting his clipboard*)
Names?

BEN
(*Saluting*)
Whitledge, Benjamin B.

WILL
(*Saluting, outdoing* BEN)
Will Stockdale, sir!

**LIEUTENANT**

Make sure they finish today. The ones chosen for Gunnery School will be leaving tomorrow, right after the Colonel's lecture.

**KING**

Yes, sir.

**LIEUTENANT**

The Colonel is taking the inspection himself. Thought you might like to know.

**KING**

Thanks for the tip, sir.

**LIEUTENANT**

(*To* BEN, WILL *and* IRVIN)
Good luck, fellows.

**WILL**

(*Saluting vigorously*)
Thank you, Lieutenant! It's been real nice bein' here! We'll sure miss yall!

**LIEUTENANT**

(*Smiles*)
Thanks, Private.
(*Salutes and exits.* WILL *looks at* BEN *for approval.*)

**KING**

(*To* IRVIN)
Why in hell does the Colonel want to come nosing around? Irvin, you better get back to the section and start slicking up the place.

IRVIN

Me?

BEN

Sergeant, can I take the clean-up detail? I'll do a real good job of it for the Colonel.

WILL

I'll lend you a hand, Ben, soon as I'm through the eye test.

KING

Lord, the eye test. (*To* IRVIN) Tell him all about it. Okay, Whitledge, you're in charge of clean-up. (*To* WILL) Have you been eating them carrots like I told you?

WILL

(*Taking carrot from pocket*)
Just one more to go.

KING

Eat fast, but chew it well—good for your eyes. And none of them wise cracks to the eye doctor. Just be nice and polite.

IRVIN

(*Crossing to* WILL)
He'll be polite, all right. (*Saluting*) "Yes, sir. No, sir. Been real nice bein' here, sir!" You're even polite to niggers, ain't you?

WILL

I don't know what you're talkin' about, Irvin.

IRVIN

That Lieutenant, that's what.

WILL

Was the Lieutenant . . . colored?
(*Glances at* BEN.)

IRVIN

What are you, blind?

WILL

I didn't notice whether he was black or white or what.
(*Glances at* BEN.)

KING

(*Looking at* WILL *with dawning horror*)
You . . . didn't . . . notice . . .

WILL

I don't notice *no color*. He might've been black or white or
yellow or even green with purple dots; it's all the same to me.
All I seen was the uniform. I never notice color *nohow.*
(WILL *looks at* BEN; BEN *grins. Door of oculist's office
opens and* FIRST CORPORAL *sticks his head out.*)

FIRST CORPORAL

Stockdale! Eye test!

KING

(*Paralyzed*)
No, no . . . it couldn't be . . .

WILL

See you at the bunk, Ben. We'll clean up good for the
Colonel, huh, Ben?

78

**BEN**

Yeah. Okay, Will.
  (WILL *exits into oculist's office.*)


**KING**

He's color-blind . . .


**IRVIN**

I don't know what you're going to do now. Half that test
is matching red and green squares.


**BEN**

Sergeant, could I look at that application a minute?


**KING**

  (*Hands him application*)
I'm doomed . . . (BEN *tears application in half and hands
pieces back to* KING) What the hell are you . . .


**BEN**

  (*Starting to exit*)
Guess I changed my mind.


**KING**

For Pete's sake, this all started from you wanting to go in
the Infantry!


**BEN**

  (*Gruffly*)
I changed my mind!
  (*Exits.*)

KING

I get all the nuts! Now what am I going to do with *that* one? If he's color-blind, Gunnery won't take him, and if they won't take him, nobody'll take him. I'm going to be a permanent latrine orderly . . .

IRVIN

Yeah . . . looks that way . . . unless . . .

KING

Unless what?

IRVIN

Unless Stockdale gets into some real trouble.

KING

What kind of trouble can he get into? He *makes* trouble.

IRVIN

He could get into plenty of trouble at the Purple Grotto.

KING

(*Horrified*)

The Purple Grotto?

IRVIN

Sure. We could invite him there . . . you know, to celebrate . . . you know—a couple of drinks . . .

KING

That's a pretty stinking idea, Irvin. After all, he ain't a bad kid. I even got to like him in a way . . .

IRVIN

His being a nice kid ain't gonna get the Captain off your
back.

KING

(*Pause*)

Yeah, let him be a nice kid on his own time.

IRVIN

We could take him there tonight. . . .

KING

(*Starting to go*)

I guess we could . . . Yeah, I guess we better. . . . Tell
you one thing though, Irvin . . . I'm glad I didn't think of it.

(*They exit. Blackout. Low-down music is heard, and
lights come up on "The Purple Grotto," a sordid den
reeking of vice and corruption.* WILL *sits at a bottle-
laden table downstage, looking about with innocent
enjoyment. A* CIGARETTE GIRL *undulates toward him.*)

CIGARETTE GIRL

Cigars, cigarettes, anything else you want to smoke . . .
(*Snakes her way around* WILL *to his other side and repeats*)
Cigars, cigarettes, anything else you want to smoke . . .

WILL

(*Flashing tobacco pouch*)

Thank you, ma'am, but I roll my own.
(*With a contemptuous sniff,* CIGARETTE GIRL *heads upstage.* KING *and* IRVIN *enter, their arms loaded with
bottles, their feet a wee bit rubbery.*)

KING

Here we are, Will. Round two.
(*Sets bottles on table.*)

WILL

I sure appreciate it. But I don't feel right my glass bein' so much bigger'n yourn.
(*Holds up enormous brandy balloon.*)

IRVIN

Guest of honor always gets the biggest glass. That's the honor. (*Raising glass*) To Will.

WILL

Again? (KING *quells him with a glance.* WILL *drinks.* KING *and* IRVIN *toss down their shots and watch, fascinated, as* WILL *drains his glass. He sets down empty glass and makes a slight grimace*) This here Scotch stuff tastes kind of sharp. I like the other stuff you give me better.

IRVIN

(*Pouring it for* WILL)

The rye.

WILL

No, the gin.
(KING *grabs gin bottle and adds it to the rye that* IRVIN *is pouring.*)

KING

How you feeling, Will?

WILL

Fine, fine.

KING

That eye doctor wouldn't tell you nothing, huh?

WILL

Nope. Seemed kind of angry most of the time.

KING

What made you think he was angry?

WILL

Well, he got sort of fussed when I was readin' this here sign they had on the wall. That was kind of hard at first 'cause they was right peculiar words like IP and GNXL and BUGLUMP.

IRVIN

You were supposed to read them letters one at a time.

WILL

Didn't make no sense that way neither.

KING

You're not drinking your rye and gin.

WILL

After this one I reckon we ought to be headin' back to Ben at the barracks. With the Colonel coming the place has got to be fixed up special.

(*Drinks, then rises.*)

KING

Now, wait a minute . . . (*Gets to his feet—sort of*) I promised you my watch, and I'm gonna give you my watch, and we gotta have several, several drinks on that!
(*Unfastens watch strap.*)

WILL

Oh, golly!
(WILL *sits.*)

KING

My mother give it to me . . . (*He's got it off now. He clears his throat*) To Will Stockdale because, because—because I'm proud of him for doing such a good job getting classified and cleaning the latrine and all . . .
(*He hands watch to* WILL *and resumes seat.*)

WILL

Thank you, thank you . . . (*Starts fastening watch, realizes he should be standing, rises*) I—I sure am glad I come into the draft! (*Snatches up his glass*) To Sergeant King! The best danged sergeant in the whole danged Air Force!
(*He drinks.* KING *and* IRVIN, *less eagerly, down their drinks.* WILL *sits, examines watch happily.*)

KING

Will . . . are you absolutely sure you never drank no whisky before?

WILL

Never no *store* whisky. Only some ole stuff that my Pa makes.

KING

Stuff that . . .

WILL

Corn likker, kind of. Corn, and grain . . . (*Sips his drink*)
. . . and kerosene . . .

KING AND IRVIN

*Kerosene!*

WILL

Just a mite. For flavorin'.
(CIGARETTE GIRL *crosses.*)

KING

(*Despondently*)
Where we gonna get kerosene?

CIGARETTE GIRL

Cigars, cigarettes, anything else you want to smoke . . .

IRVIN

(*Thrusting dollar bill into her tray*)
Here's some lighter fluid. . . .

KING

He *wants* kerosene, he *gets* kerosene!
(IRVIN *fires a few squirts of fluid into* WILL's *glass.*
KING *and* IRVIN *sit raptly as* WILL *lifts glass, inspects
it, sips, and savors the aftertaste.*)

WILL

It's familiar. (KING *and* IRVIN *groan*) Hey, there's an Infantry man! Hey, Infantry! (*A burly* INFANTRY PRIVATE *stag-
gers to their table.*)

INFANTRY

Hi, Jack!

WILL

Have a drink! We're celebratin'!

INFANTRY

(*Pulling up a chair*)
Thanks a lot. I do not mind if I do.

WILL

(*To* KING *and* IRVIN)
Let's drink one to the Infantry.

INFANTRY

(*Grabbing* WILL's *upraised glass*)
To the Infantry! (*He drinks, stiffens, sets glass on table, shakes his head*) Smooth . . . Say, I never seen fly-boys so nice to the Infantry.

WILL

Well, heck, this is the Air Age, and you're our helpers, ain't you?

KING AND IRVIN

Will, Will . . .

INFANTRY

Your what?

WILL

Our helpers. And don't think we don't appreciate it.

INFANTRY

Listen, you guys got it easier than anybody, even the Navy!

IRVIN

For your information they drill us fifteen miles every day!

INFANTRY

Twenty miles, we drill! When it rains, twenty-five!

KING

Do you have to put up with all the stupid kid officers we do?

IRVIN

And sergeants . . . we got the roughest, toughest, mean-est sergeants in the whole service!

INFANTRY

Go on, you don't know what a tough sergeant is till you've been in the infantry!

IRVIN

Ain't nobody tougher than my sergeant! He's *tough!*

KING

I sure am!

WILL

Now, Sergeant, I wouldn't say that.

KING

I'm a louse, ain't I, Irvin?

IRVIN

Yes, sir, you are.

KING

Thanks, Irvin.

INFANTRY

I don't know, you look like a pretty decent Joe to me.

KING

(*Rising*)

You take that back!

INFANTRY

All right, I'll bet you five bucks *I'm* a bigger louse than you.
And I'm just a private!

IRVIN

Put up or shut up.
(*Throws money on table.*)

INFANTRY

(*To* KING)

What's a bigger louse than a louse that'll drink your booze
and then punch you in the guts?

IRVIN

Put up or shut up!

INFANTRY

Sure.

(INFANTRY *punches* KING *in the stomach.* KING *doubles
up.* INFANTRY *turns to* IRVIN, *who violates the Mar-
quess of Queensberry Rules with his right knee. A
brawl ensues, in the midst of which* WILL *attempts
to disengage* KING.)

WILL

Sergeant, I think we better go home now. Ben's waitin'
for me to—

KING

(*Strangling someone*)
Go on away! You're drunk!

WILL

No I ain't. My fingers is a mite tingly, but—

KING

Go 'way!

(*With bottles flying and a siren wailing, the lights
fade out on "The Purple Grotto" as* WILL, *in a pin-spot,
reluctantly comes downstage. He addresses the audience.*)

WILL

Well, I finally figgered I better quit bein' a wet blanket
and stop spoilin' the Sergeant's fun. So . . . much as I hated
to miss the fun myself—you know, quit a party early and the
best things happen after you're gone—I went on back to the
barracks 'cause I had a lot to do before the Colonel come.
(*An* AIR FORCE POLICEMAN *rushes across.*)

AIR FORCE POLICEMAN

Hey! Which way's that Purple Grotto?

WILL

Right down yonder there. (*To audience*) There's a thirsty
fellow for you! Well, anyhow, I went on back to the barracks
and give Ben a hand with the cleanin'. And afterwards, when

everyone was asleep, I got me some nails and a board and some wires and I fixed up somethin' special for the Colonel. Then in the mornin', right before inspection, I give it the finishin' touches.

(*Lights come up on barracks set.* WILL *takes a wire-entangled board from within latrine door and stands straightening the wires as* BEN *approaches.*)

BEN

What you been doing in there?

WILL

Fixin' up somethin' special. It ain't every day a Colonel inspects.

BEN

I sure wish the Sergeant was here.

WILL

He'll show up. Sergeant King ain't gonna miss no inspection if he can help it.

BEN

The heck he ain't. Here comes the Captain now—and the Colonel!

WILL

Oh, golly.

BEN

Who's going to report?

WILL

You're in charge.

**BEN**

Me? Oh! (*Rehearsing salute*) Barracks ready for inspection, sir. Barracks ready for inspection, sir . . .

**WILL**

Now mind, when you throw open this door, holler "attention" just as loud as you can!

**BEN**

(*Preoccupied*)

Yeah, yeah . . . (*Closes latrine door*) Barracks ready for inspection, sir. Barracks ready . . . (CAPTAIN *and* COLONEL *enter in conversation.* BEN, *between latrine and* KING's *room, keeps rehearsing until officers are upon him. He calls to* INDUCTEES *in back*) Ten-shun! (*Saluting officers*) Barracks ready for inspection, sir!

(OFFICERS, *flinching at his vehemence, return salute.* WILL, *in latrine, is placing the wired board on the floor before commodes, fussing with wires, etc.*)

**CAPTAIN**

Where's Sergeant King?

**BEN**

I don't know, sir, but (*Saluting*) the barracks are ready for inspection, sir!

**CAPTAIN**

(*Saluting mechanically*)

All right, all right . . . (*To Colonel*) Sir, before we go any further, I'd like you to take a look at this latrine. There's a man in this barracks whose latrine work is quite surprising.

(BEN *flings open latrine door.*)

### BEN

*Ten-shun!*

   (*Up comes* WILL'*s arm in a snappy salute, down stomps his foot, up fly the toilet seats; clattering, banging, quivering at attention.*)

### WILL

Latrine ready for inspection, sir!

   (OFFICERS *recoil through the door, then peer in again timorously. They enter latrine, hesitantly approach the commodes. The seats waver.* WILL *gives the board a further push and the seats regain their precision.* OFFICERS *turn their dumbfounded gaze at* WILL.)

### WILL

Latrine ready for inspection, sir!

### CAPTAIN

   (*Dazedly returns salute.* WILL *drops his hand*)
What is . . . the *idea* behind this?

### WILL

Welcomin' the Colonel, sir.

### CAPTAIN

   (*To Colonel*)
I'm sorry, sir.

### COLONEL

It's all right, Captain . . . I've been welcomed in many ways; with ticker-tape, with waving flags, the women of a French village once threw rosebuds at me . . . But this . . . this . . .

*(Shaking his head, he and* CAPTAIN *leave latrine and exit into barracks proper. The clatter of the falling seats speeds them.)*

WILL

*(Joining* BEN *outside latrine)*
They didn't hardly inspect the latrine at all.
*(*KING *comes staggering in, looking back cautiously over his shoulder. He is a bruised and battered wreck, his uniform in shreds. His stripes are hanging by a thread, literally and figuratively.)*

BEN

*(As* KING *totters up)*
Sergeant!

KING

Lieutenant there . . . almost spotted me . . .

WILL

You all right?

KING

I'm not sure . . .

WILL

Where's Irvin?

KING

The M.P.s got him.

WILL

Golly . . .

COLONEL
*(Off)*

Excellent! Excellent!

KING

*(Wide-eyed)*

The Colonel?
(WILL *nods excitedly.*)

BEN

They inspected the latrine already!

WILL

Watch out for the treadle!
(KING *ducks into latrine.* COLONEL *and* CAPTAIN *reappear.* CAPTAIN *opens door of* KING'S *room.* COLONEL *pokes his head in.*)

COLONEL

Excellent! Excellent! (*To* BEN) Were you in charge during your sergeant's absence?

BEN

Yes, sir. Complete charge.

COLONEL

Captain, I think you should make a note of this man's name.
(KING *is examining himself in the mirror.*)

CAPTAIN

Yes indeed, sir. What is it, Private?

BEN

Private Ben Whitledge, sir!

(KING *backs away from mirror to get better look at himself. He steps on the treadle. The seats fly up with a horrendous clatter. As he turns to see what the clatter is he steps off the treadle and the seats crash down again.*)

CAPTAIN

(*When the noise subsides*)

What was that again?

(*Produces pencil and note pad.*)

BEN

Whitledge, sir. W—H—I—T—

(KING *has been cautiously tiptoeing toward seats to examine them. He steps on the treadle. The seats fly up. As he backs up, they crash down.*)

COLONEL

What in blazes?

CAPTAIN

What's going on in there?

(COLONEL *and* CAPTAIN *move to latrine door.* WILL *blocks it.*)

WILL

Latrine's out of order, sir. You'll have to use the one next door.

(CAPTAIN *gestures* WILL *aside, flings open the door.* KING *retreats to the far corner of the latrine and attempts a salute, but with the hangover and the shock he can't quite make it.*)

**95**

**CAPTAIN**

*This* is the barracks sergeant!

**KING**

How are ya, sir. . . .

**CAPTAIN**

All slicked up for inspection! (KING *withers. Pause*) Explain!

**KING**

Explain . . . uh . . . mm . . . Well, sir . . . I went to a movie last night. And there were these . . . *eight infantrymen* sitting behind me. And they took to cussing the Air Force, and saying how our officers wasn't as . . . understanding . . . as Infantry officers.

**COLONEL**

So you fought them. All night long.

**KING**

Yes sir. It was awful.

**CAPTAIN**

What was the name of the movie?

**KING**

The movie . . . ?

**CAPTAIN**

The movie!

**KING**

Uh . . . Forward March . . . American Battalion . . . of the Air . . . in the Wild Blue . . . It was a sneak preview.

**COLONEL**

I don't know how this man ever got *on* my base, Captain, but he certainly isn't going to remain here, corrupting new airmen with his—hideous example. Ship him out!

**CAPTAIN**

There's a group leaving today for Gunnery School.

**COLONEL**

Splendid! General Bush can always use another private.

**KING**

Private?

**COLONEL**

*(Plucks dangling stripes from* KING's *arms and drops them to the floor)*
Private!
      *(*KING *clasps his arms as though wounded.* COLONEL *and* CAPTAIN *leave latrine.* BEN *confronts them outside.)*

**BEN**

That was Whitledge, sir. W—H—I—T—L—

**CAPTAIN**

Whitledge, eh? This is going on your record, Whitledge! This is going on everybody's record!

(COLONEL *and* CAPTAIN *exit furiously.* WILL *enters latrine.*)

KING

(*Pointing at commodes, flapping his hand*)
Something special for the Colonel . . .

WILL
(*Nods*)
You ain't a sergeant no more?

KING

No I ain't a sergeant no more! I'm a private, a forty-five-year-old private!

WILL

Oh, gosh, I—

BEN
(*Coming to door*)
He's putting it on my record . . .

WILL

Gosh, Ben, I didn't . . .

KING

There's a silver lining to this cloud, by God! You're staying here, but I'm going to Gunnery School, a thousand miles away!
(*Comes out of latrine.* WILL *and* BEN *follow.*)

WILL

Sergeant . . .

KING

Private!

WILL

I ain't stayin' here. I'm goin' to Gunnery School, just like you.

KING

They . . . took you?

WILL

It's right on the bulletin board. It was your helpin' that done it for me.

KING

No . . .

WILL
(Hesitantly)

We're gonna be together.

KING

Now listen, I've had all I can take, you understand? You and him be together; leave me out of it!

WILL

But we're buddies.

KING

*Buddies?*

WILL

Last night you said you was proud of me . . .

KING

I was drunk! I didn't know what I was saying!

99

WILL

You give me your watch . . .

KING

I was drunk!

WILL

Not when you set me in charge of this latrine!

KING

Oh, my God! (*To* BEN) You tell him! Maybe you can get through!

BEN

Cleaning the latrine isn't a good job, Will. It's the worst job there is. It's a punishment job.

WILL

(*Turns slowly from* BEN *to* KING)

It is?

(*Begins unfastening watch strap.*)

KING

(*Uncomfortable now*)

Now do you understand? There's your buddy. Make some trouble for *him* for a change. (WILL *holds out the watch.* KING *hesitates, then crosses and snatches it from him. To* BEN) You glad now you tore up your transfer?

(*He exits into his room. There is a moment of silence.*)

WILL

You tore up your transfer, Ben?

**BEN**

(*Inching away*)
It was just an application, that's all.

**WILL**

To the Infantry!

**BEN**

(*Heading for wings. More for himself than for* WILL)
Nothing would've come of it!

**WILL**

I didn't know you done that. I'll make it up to you, honest
I will. Ben . . .
(BEN *stops, turns, holds himself in check.*)

**BEN**

I got to go pack for Gunnery School . . .
(*He exits. After a moment,* WILL *turns downstage,
looking at floor. He becomes aware of the audience
watching.*)

**WILL**

I didn't realize . . . honest . . . I was just . . .
(*He turns, putting his back toward them. The lights
fade slowly.*)

**Curtain**

# ACT TWO

# ACT TWO

*WILL comes on in front of the "Meeting Hall" curtain. He holds a slip of paper in his hand.*

### WILL

Feels right good to move around after settin' still so long, don't it? (*Glances at slip of paper*) Uh . . . Preacher says that Mrs. Henry Calhoun couldn't find one of her shoes when yall went out for that orange drink. Would all them around her look under you and if it's there just pass it on back to her? Thank you. (*Pockets paper*) Let's see . . . where was I—oh yeh. Well, the three of us—Ben and Sergeant King and me—we went to Gunnery School together, like the Three Musketeers. Only to be real honest, we warn't really much like the Three Musketeers; it was more like three fellows that two of 'em warn't talkin' with one of 'em any more'n they could help. Anyway, after Gunnery School they put me and Ben on the same flight crew, because they put you accordin' to how you come out in the class, and we was the bottom two. Sergeant King, though, he come out on top. He did. The instructors said they never seen nothin' like it. It was just as if he had copies of the tests before they give them. He done so good that General Bush—he's kind of like the principal of the school—General Bush give him his stripes back and made him his orderly, and an orderly is kind of important; it's like a right-hand man . . . or an assistant . . . or a helper . . . Well, it's really more like a servant is what it is. Everybody

105

said this crew Ben and me was on was the worst one on the base, on account of the officers was all from the bottom of their class too. The other crews had a nickname for our'n, only I can't say it with the ladies here. In fact I don't think I could say it with the *men* here. Ben and me, though, we went on most of the missions; it warn't much trouble and there warn't nothin' else to do anyhow. (*"Meeting Hall" curtain rises on an airstrip. A medium-sized plane stands ready for take-off, a mounting ladder reaching up into its underbelly.*) Ben was pretty upset about it. You know how he is.

    (BEN, *in flying gear, comes striding in from left.*)

#### BEN

If this ain't the sorriest crew on the whole danged base! We're supposed to take off five minutes ago, and do you know what? Every one of our officers would still be fast asleep if I hadn't gone and shook them awake! What a crew!

#### WILL

It's just that they ain't used to gettin' up at three in the mornin', Ben.

#### BEN

All the other planes got off on time except ours. These officers are a disgrace to the Air Force!

#### WILL

Now, Ben, they ain't so bad. Easy goin', that's all.

#### BEN

All I know is that if you're going to fly a plane you ought to be awake first. I'm going aboard.

    (*He climbs the ladder into the plane.*)

WILL

(*Calling after him*)

Here's Lieutenant Bridges now, Ben. (LIEUTENANT BRIDGES *enters sleepily, his parachute at half-mast.* WILL *salutes smartly*) Good mornin', Lieutenant Bridges!

BRIDGES

Good morning, Lieutenant Bridges . . .
(*He continues across stage somnambulistically.* WILL *calls after him.*)

WILL

The plane's right here, sir. (BRIDGES, *without stopping, turns back and drags himself up the ladder and into the plane*) That's the pilot. Easy goin' fellow. (LIEUTENANT GARDELLA *and* LIEUTENANT KENDALL *enter. They pause a few feet onstage and* GARDELLA *helps* KENDALL *adjust his parachute straps*) This here is Lieutenant Kendall, the engineer, and Lieutenant Gardella, the co-pilot. Lieutenant Kendall ain't quite got the hang of puttin' on a parachute yet. (*The pair approach.* WILL *salutes*) Good morning, sirs!

KENDALL AND GARDELLA

(*Saluting*)

Good morning . . .

WILL

Lieutenant Gardella.
(GARDELLA *stops.* KENDALL *exits into plane.*)

GARDELLA

Yes?

WILL

Sir, would it be all right if I come up to the front of the plane for a while and watch what yall do up there?

GARDELLA

Sorry. Only crew members allowed on board.

WILL

I'm a crew member, sir.

GARDELLA

You are?

WILL

Yes, sir. I been on the crew for close on to a month now. Is it okay if I come up front and—

GARDELLA

Sure. Sure. Come on up. There ain't much to see though. All I do is let the wheels up after we take off and let them down again when we're ready to land.

WILL

That might be nice. Thank you, sir.

GARDELLA

I *knew* I'd seen you *some place.*
(*Exits into plane.* WILL *takes parachute from behind ladder, puts it on during following.*)

WILL

(*To audience*)
I think he really knowed who I was. It's just the sleep ain't wore off yet. You see, we never had to go up this early before.

This here mission is we're supposed to fly to Denver, Colorado, and when we get to Denver, Colorado, we're supposed to turn around and fly back again. That's the biggest mission we got so far. Usually, all they ask is for us to get the plane up off'n the ground and keep it up for half an hour or so without smackin' into nothin'.

(LIEUTENANT COVER *comes scurrying on, his arms loaded with maps, sextants, slide rules, books, etc. He climbs the ladder, muttering a hasty inventory, oblivious of* WILL's *salute.*)

#### COVER

Maps . . . sextant . . . slide rule . . . scale . . . dramamine . . . I forgot the—No, here it is.
(*He is gone.*)

#### WILL

That's Lieutenant Cover, the navigator. He's the serious one of the bunch. (*Glances at his wrist watch but he doesn't have one. Rubs wrist*) Well, I guess I'll just get on the—
(SERGEANT KING *and two* MECHANICS *enter.* KING *wears a staff armband and carries a clipboard. Engines rev up as* MECHANICS *busy themselves underneath the plane.*)

#### KING

(*To* MECHANICS)
Get this one off and we can all go back to sleep.

#### WILL

Hey, look at you! An armband and a writin' board and everythin'!

#### KING

All right, get this plane off on the double.

WILL

We can't. Everyone ain't here yet. The radio operator and the front gunner—

KING

You heard me, get moving!

WILL

How come we're goin' up so early?

KING

To break the sound barrier. You gotta sneak up on it when nobody's looking.
(GENERAL BUSH *enters.*)

BUSH

Oh, there you are, Sergeant. Is this the last of them?

KING

Yes, General.

BUSH

Fine. That does it for tonight. Don't disturb me unless there's a big emergency. Breakfast a little later than usual, I think . . .

KING

Yes, sir. What about your eggs, sir?

BUSH

My eggs? What eggs?

KING

For breakfast. Poached or scrambled?

BUSH

Scrambled, I think . . . nice and loose. No, no . . . poached.

KING

Yes, sir, poached.

BUSH

Poached. I feel like poached.

WILL

Scrambled is tastier, sir. Especially with chitlins.

KING

Get on that plane!

BUSH

Chitlins?

WILL

Yes, sir, at home we always have scrambled eggs with chitlins.

BUSH

Poached!
(*Exits.*)

KING

Yes, sir! (*To* WILL) Can't you keep your mouth shut? Scrambled with chitlins!

WILL

A bit of red pepper helps.

KING

Get on that plane!

WILL

*(Climbing ladder)*

Sure, Sergeant.

VOICE ON P.A.

Sergeant King! Sergeant King! Report to General Bush immediately. *(Incredulous)* With chitlins?

*Blackout*

*(The roar of the engines grows louder. Clouds are seen, and running lights blinking in a rhythmic pattern. Lights come up on a cross-section of the plane in flight. In front, BRIDGES and GARDELLA are seated at the controls, asleep. Behind them, KENDALL sits by his needles and gauges, asleep. Farther back, COVER is at his work table, frantically operating six instruments at once. Toward the rear of the plane, BEN sits reading a comic book. WILL is peering at the audience from the tail blister. After a moment the sound of the engines fades low and WILL moves forward. He crouches beside BEN.)*

WILL

I got my penknife. Want to play mumbly-peg?

BEN

That's a kid's game.
*(Turns a page of his comic book.)*

**WILL**

We could play for money. (*No comment from* BEN.) Well, I guess I'll go see what they do up front.

**BEN**

We're supposed to stay at our stations.

**WILL**

I asked Lieutenant Gardella. He said it was all right. Want to come along?
> (BEN *shakes his head.* WILL *hesitates, then moves forward.* COVER *is working like a man possessed; marking charts, measuring, drawing circles, searching for instruments and papers.* WILL *watches him, fascinated.*)

**COVER**
> (*Talking to himself*)

Compass, compass . . . ah . . . mmm . . . now . . . scale. Where's the . . . (*Snaps his fingers*) Ruler, ruler . . . (WILL *hands it to him*) Ah . . . there . . . (*Copying data from various sheets of paper onto central sheet*) Ground speed . . . mmm . . . air speed . . . mmm . . . wind direction— Wind direction, wind direction . . .
> (*Searches furiously through papers.* WILL, *behind him, licks his forefinger and holds it up. He taps* COVER.)

**WILL**

Wind's comin' from that way, sir.
> (*Points forward.*)

**COVER**
> (*Turning*)

Dead ahead?

WILL

Yes, sir.


COVER

(*Returning to charts*)

Then something's wrong with the compass. We're supposed to be . . . that couldn't . . . (*He is beginning to get a
bit desperate.* WILL *watches him for a moment, then heads
forward*) Now wait a minute, let's start all over again. If we
took off at 0315 . . .


WILL

(*Stepping over Kendall's outstretched legs*)

Excuse me, sir . . . (*He comes up behind* BRIDGES *and* GAR-
DELLA, *who are slumped over the steering wheels*) Howdy,
sirs!

(*They sit bolt upright and whirl around in their
chairs.*)


GARDELLA

It's all right, George; he's one of the crew.


BRIDGES

Lord! Don't come sneaking up on people, fella.


WILL

Sorry, sir. Just wanted to watch what yall do up here.

(*Pause.* BRIDGES *and* GARDELLA *resume their sleeping
positions.*)


BRIDGES

Automatic pilot.


WILL

You already let up the wheels?

GARDELLA

Hell, yes.

WILL

Shucks.

BRIDGES

What do yall do in back?

WILL

Oh, nothin' much. I mostly look out the blister and sweep up a little (*Pause. Apprehensively*) You don't have to guide this here thing?

BRIDGES

Automatic. Everything's automatic. Every little ole thing.

GARDELLA

You come back when we're ready to land and you can watch me let down the wheels.

BRIDGES

It's a real spectacle.

GARDELLA

I do it all with one hand.

WILL

Well, thank you, sir. Guess I'll go look out the blister some. (*Pause*) Good night. (*He heads for the rear of the plane, stepping over* KENDALL's *legs . . .*) Excuse me, sir.

> (*. . . and stopping behind* COVER, *who is staring straight ahead with a stoned expression, his hands flat on the work table.*)

COVER

We're off our course.

WILL

We are?

COVER

If we're heading straight into a south wind then we can't be going west, can we? (WILL *licks his finger and holds it up*) Are they in contact with the base up there?

WILL

Well, no . . .

COVER

(*Putting on earphones*)
What the hell *are* they doing?

WILL

Well, sir, you might say they're kind of sleepin'.

COVER

Sleeping! Navigator to pilot, navigator to pilot. Over. (BRIDGES *lifts one hand and pulls down earphones without opening his eyes. He holds one phone to ear.*) Navigator to pilot, navigator to pilot. Over.

BRIDGES

Pilot to navigator. Fred, I wish you wouldn't call me once we're off the ground. Over.

COVER

I just thought you might like to know that we're heading for Mexico, that's all. Over.

**BRIDGES**

Now Fred, everything is automatic and you know it. Every time we go off on a mission you start fussing with those maps and things, and all you do is confuse everybody. Over.

**COVER**

Well, for your information we got a south wind and we're heading straight into it and we're supposed to be going west. Over.

**BRIDGES**

(*Extends his toe and does something with the instrument panel*)
All right. I just moved us up ninety degrees. Are you happy? Over and out.
(*Hangs up earphones.*)

**COVER**

I don't see why you guys should get to sleep when I have to work like a dog back here. None of *my* instruments are automatic and they're pretty damn complicated, let me tell you. Over. Navigator to pilot, navigator to ... Damn! (*Hangs up earphones*) Sometimes I think he doesn't take a serious attitude.

**WILL**

I noticed that.

**COVER**

Now let's see . . . moved us up ninety degrees . . . wind from the south . . . flying since 0315 hours . . .
(WILL *retreats toward rear of plane.*)

BEN

(*Not looking up from comic book*)
Taking an awful long time to get to Denver, Colorado.
What are they doing up there?

WILL

Oh, you'd be right proud of them, Ben! They're workin'
real hard; navigatin' and steerin' and engineerin' and all.

BEN

Yeah, I'll bet.

WILL

They're about as good a crew as you can find, when they're
sober like this.

(*Lights fade, engine sound rises, clouds and running
lights are seen. After a moment, interior lights come
up again.* BEN *is sleeping,* WILL *is sweeping,* COVER *is
shouting frantically into his microphone.*)

COVER

Navigator to pilot, navigator to pilot, over! Navigator to
pilot, navigator to pilot!

BRIDGES

(*Snatching earphones*)
Fred, what the hell's the matter with you?

COVER

We're over the Gulf of Mexico, you idiot!

BRIDGES

Now, Fred, how can we be over the Gulf of Mexico when there's a city below us half the size of New York?

COVER

You want to come back here and check the maps? I figured our position by dead reckoning and we're smack-dab in the middle of the Gulf of Mexico!

BRIDGES

Well, by God, I can see, can't I? I can look right out the window and *see*, can't I?

KENDALL

(*Taking earphones, partially awake*)
Engineer to pilot. Are we lost again?

COVER

No, Kendall, we know exactly where we are. Smack dab in the middle of the Gulf of Mexico.

BRIDGES

There ain't any towns in the middle of the Gulf of Mexico!

GARDELLA

Maybe we're across the Gulf already.

COVER

You stay out of this, Gardella!

KENDALL

(*A bit surprised*)
Hey, fellows. Number two engine is dead.

**GARDELLA AND COVER**

Oh Lord!

**BRIDGES**

Prepare for landing!

**COVER**

This is *not* a seaplane!

**BRIDGES**

Cover, will you please look out the ever-loving window. What do you think that is down there?

**GARDELLA**

Wait a minute, wait a minute! That gunner fellow said he was going to watch from the blister . . . Co-pilot to rear gunner, co-pilot to rear gunner, over. Co-pilot to rear gunner . . .

(*A red light blinks in rear of plane.* WILL *goes to it, takes earphones.*)

**WILL**

Howdy. Over.

**GARDELLA**

Hey, you seen anything below that might've been a body of water?

**WILL**

No sir, I ain't seen nothin'. I been sweepin' up.

**BRIDGES**

What the hell's the radio operator doing? Pilot to radio operator, pilot to radio operator, over.

**120**

GARDELLA

Co-pilot to radio operator. Over.

COVER

Navigator to radio operator, over.

WILL

Rear gunner to everybody. Radio operator missed the plane. Over.

OFFICERS

Oh, no!

BRIDGES

Listen, rear gunner, get on the radio and see if you can find out where we are. This is an emergency. Over.

WILL

It is?

COVER

(*Tossing aside earphones, gathering up maps*)
We know *exactly* where we are!
(*Storms toward the front of plane.*)

WILL

Hey, sir, you ought to give the job to the other gunner! I reckon he'd be just about the best danged radio operator in the whole danged Air Force!

BRIDGES

(*Over him*)
All right, get him on it.

WILL

(*Going right on*)
He's a real smart fellow and right military-like. His whole family been—

BRIDGES

ALL RIGHT! Just get *somebody* on the damn radio! Over and out!

WILL

Roger!
(*Hangs up earphones, drops broom and goes to* BEN)

COVER

(*Thrusting maps over* BRIDGES' *shoulder*)
You want to see the map? Here's the Gulf of Mexico right here!
(BRIDGES *pushes him away.*)

WILL

(*Shaking* BEN *gently*)
Ben? Hey, Ben. Wake up, Ben.

BEN

What . . .

WILL

It's an emergency! We're lost and Lieutenant Bridges wants you to be the radio operator and find out where we are! It's up to you to save the plane and us and everythin'!

BEN

Me?

122

**WILL**

They heared what a good soldier you was.
(*Drags* BEN *to his feet and leads him to radio equipment.*)

**BEN**

Me? . . . Oh golly . . . oh Lord . . .

**WILL**

(*Picks up pamphlet, looks at it*)
Here's some instructions . . .

**BEN**

(*Sitting at equipment*)
Good. Read them off. I'll operate and you'll be my assistant.
(*Puts on earphones.*)

**WILL**

Assistant? Yes, sir!
(*He opens pamphlet, while* BEN *straightens his jacket, sitting proudly erect.*)

**KENDALL**

Watch out! Those are mountains there!

**GARDELLA**

Pull up! Pull up! *Pull up!*

**BRIDGES**

How do you pull up with only one engine, Mr. Rickenbacker?

**GARDELLA**

*You're* the pilot, Mr. Lindbergh.

COVER

There aren't any mountains on the map . . .

WILL

(*Reading with difficulty*)
Con-grat-u-lations. As an Air Force radio operator yours
is one of the most important jobs in—

BEN

Skip that part. Get to the instructions.

WILL

Yes, sir. (*Turns several pages, skimming them as he does
so. Reads again*) Important notice. The taxpayers of the
United States paid their hard-earned—

BEN

The instructions! How to operate it.

WILL

(*Turns several more pages, which brings him to the end of
the pamphlet. Shows* BEN)
Just half a page. (*Squints, reads*) One. Turn the power
switch to the on position.

BEN

Here, this one. This is it. (*Pause*) Here goes . . . (*Turns
switch. Lights appear on equipment*) Hey . . .

WILL

How about that!

**BRIDGES**

Pilot to radio operator. You getting anything back there? Over.

**BEN**

(*As baritone as he can get*)
Radio operator to pilot, sir! Roger! Wilco! We're working on it. Over! How about that?

**WILL**

Pretty good! Two. Turn . . . turn . . . O-S-C-I-L-L-A-T-O-R . . .

**BEN**

Oscillator.

**WILL**

Turn—what-you-just-said—control knob to tran . . . tran . . . T-R-A-N-S—

**BEN**

(*Taking off earphones, rising*)
Here. You operate, I'll read. (*Gives* WILL *earphones, takes pamphlet.*)

**WILL**

But they give you the job, Ben!

**BEN**

Go on! I got to think of the good of the outfit!
(WILL *sits, puts on earphones. During following* BEN *strips off parachute, up-ends it beside* WILL *and sits on it. He reads with less difficulty than* WILL.)

125

BEN

Two. Turn oscillator control knob—I think that's the big one there—to transmission frequency desired.

WILL

(*Turns knob*)

What frequency we desire?

BEN

Oh . . . I'll leave it up to you.

WILL

(*Makes careful adjustment*)

All righty . . .

BEN

Three. Adjust knob B so as to obtain minimum impedance.

WILL

(*Pause*)

Ben, listen, we got a little radio on the porch back home, and when it won't start, Pa spits in the back of it and whomps it a good one. Works every time. (BEN *shrugs noncommittally.* WILL *leans over radio, spits in the back of it and whomps it a good one. A red bulb on top lights up*) There y'are! She's workin'! (*Picking up microphone*) Hello? Hello? I don't hear nothin'.

BEN

You got to keep saying it over and over again until somebody picks up your signal.

WILL

Hello? Hello? Hello?

**BRIDGES**

I told you I'd find an airport!

**GARDELLA, KENDALL AND COVER**

*That's a drive-in movie! Pull up!*
>    (*Lights begin to fade, light on* WILL *and* BEN *going last.*)

**WILL**

Hello? Hello?

**BEN**

If you get somebody, be careful what you say. They might be the enemy.

**WILL**

What enemy?

**BEN**

I don't know, but be careful.

**WILL**

Hello? Hello? (*Spits at microphone*) Anybody out there? Hello?

>    (*Fade-out complete. Lights come up on a sandbagged bunker at extreme right of stage.* GENERAL POLLARD, *the ramrod type of officer, stands scanning the horizon with powerful binoculars. His aide, a* LIEUTENANT, *is seated at a bank of radio, telephone and radar equipment. A* SENATOR *approaches from right, where there apparently is an extension of the bunker.*)

**SENATOR**

Did you just hear an airplane?

POLLARD

An airplane? You're joking, Senator.

SENATOR

No, no, I'm perfectly serious.

POLLARD

My dear Senator, a plane couldn't conceivably slip in here unless they had Lindbergh for pilot and Rickenbacker for co-pilot. Ha, ha, ha. When General Pollard is in charge of an operation, safety is the prime consideration. You can mention that in your report to your Committee if you'd like.

SENATOR

I could have sworn I heard engines . . .

POLLARD

(*Ushering the* SENATOR *off right*)
The desert plays strange tricks on the ear. Auditory mirages, so to speak.

LIEUTENANT

Excuse me, sir, but I'm getting a very odd signal here. Listen . . .

RADIO

Tphhh . . . tphhh . . . tphhh . . . tphhh . . .

POLLARD

Hmmm, that *is* odd . . . Sounds like somebody spitting.

BEN'S VOICE

(*Filter. Off mike*)
Okay, Will. Try again.

WILL'S VOICE
*(Filter. Off mike)*
Yes, sir. *(On)* Hello? Hello? Anybody there? Hello?

POLLARD
*(Seizing a microphone)*
Hello.

WILL'S VOICE
Hello?

POLLARD
Hello!

WILL'S VOICE
HOWDY! *(Off mike)* Ben, I got somebody!

POLLARD
Who are you? Where are you?

WILL'S VOICE
*(Off mike)*
Ben, he wants to know who we are.

POLLARD
Answer me, dammit. Who the hell are you?

WILL'S VOICE
*(Off mike)*
He talks like an American, Ben.

POLLARD
Who are you?

WILL'S VOICE

Ben says, first who are you?

POLLARD

This is Command Post, "Operation Prometheus." Are you in . . . an airplane?

WILL'S VOICE

Sure are!

POLLARD

Oh Lord . . .

LIEUTENANT

I've got them on the PPI scope, sir! They're heading straight for the tower!

POLLARD

Oh my God!

WILL'S VOICE

Is this the Gulf of Mexico?

POLLARD

No, you idiot! (*To* LIEUTENANT) Send word to stop the detonator!

LIEUTENANT

It's too late, sir! Zero minus three!

WILL'S VOICE

Where'd you say we was?

130

POLLARD

You're right over Yucca Flats! Now listen to me, you turn
that plane around and go right back where you came from!
This minute!

LIEUTENANT

(*Pointing to radarscope*)
There they are! See? Straight toward the tower!

WILL'S VOICE

Ben says sorry, our orders come from General Bush. Gotta
do like he says.

POLLARD

Eugene Bush?

WILL'S VOICE

Our Commandin' General. Short fellow with a mustache.

POLLARD

I might have known. Get a line through to that idiot! I'll
kill him for this! (LIEUTENANT *picks up the telephone, ad libs
putting through of call.* POLLARD *speaks into microphone
again*) All right now, I don't care what Ben says or what
Eugene Bush said. I'm a General too, in the U.S. Infantry—

WILL'S VOICE

The Infantry?

POLLARD

Yes! I'm ordering you to turn that plane around this in-
stant! You're heading straight into . . . Hello? Hello? Oh
God, I lost them! (*He twirls radio dials furiously.* SENATOR
*enters from right*) Hello? Hello?

SENATOR

Has something gone wrong?

POLLARD

No, no, no! Everything's fine. Lieutenant, help the Senator into his ear plugs and blinders. (LIEUTENANT *does so and through the rest of the scene the* SENATOR, *now deaf, smiles benignly in anticipation*) Where's Bush? Where is he?

LIEUTENANT

I've put the call through, sir. (*Looks at watch*) Zero minus two.

POLLARD

(*Taking telephone*)
Hello? Hello? Hello? Hello?

> (*At the other side of the stage, lights come up on a corner of* BUSH's *office.* KING *stands behind desk, telephone in hand.* BUSH *enters.*)

KING

(*Overlapping* POLLARD)
Hello? Hello? Hello?—Here he is now, sir!
(BUSH *grabs phone from* KING.)

BUSH

Bush here.

POLLARD

Eugene? This is Vernon Pollard!

BUSH

Vernon! How are you, old boy?

POLLARD

You've sabotaged my operation, you miserable idiot! You were ordered to send your planes as far away as you could, and one of them is right here!

BUSH

I sent them away, Vernon! I sent them to Denver!

POLLARD

I don't care where you sent them! What's wrong with your communication?

BUSH

What's wrong with your security measures?

POLLARD

Shut up and listen! I 'm trying to re-establish radio contact. What kind of idiot radio operators did you *put* in those planes?

BUSH

(*To* KING)

What kind of idiot radio operators did you *put* in those planes?

POLLARD

I'll skin you for this, Eugene.

LIEUTENANT

Sir, I've got that signal again!

POLLARD

Hold it! Don't move, Eugene!

RADIO

Tphhhh . . . tphhhh . . . tphhhh . . . tphhhh . . .

WILL'S VOICE

Hello? Hello?

POLLARD

*(Seizing microphone)*
Hello! Listen! Here's your General Bush!

WILL'S VOICE

*(Off mike)*
He's got General Bush there, Ben!

POLLARD

*(Into phone)*
Eugene, I'm putting the telephone next to the microphone.
Tell this idiot to turn back!
*(He holds telephone and microphone together.)*

BUSH

Hello? Who is this?

WILL'S VOICE

Private Stockdale, sir.

BUSH

This is General Bush, Stockdale.

KING

Stockdale!
*(Starts for door.)*

BUSH

Don't move, King! Tell your pilot to reverse course immediately, Stockdale. You're in extreme danger.

WILL'S VOICE

Roger, sir! Wilco. (*Pause*) Ben says how do we know you're General Bush?

BUSH

What? I can't go up there and identify myself!

KING

(*Frantically*)

Tell him Sergeant King will give him his watch!

BUSH

What?

KING

It's the only way, sir!

BUSH

Sergeant King will give you his watch!

WILL'S VOICE

He will!

BUSH

I *think* so . . .

WILL'S VOICE

That's good enough for me! Ben, tell Lieutenant Bridges to reverse course!

LIEUTENANT

(*Over this*)

Twenty seconds, sir!

POLLARD

(*Looking at radarscope*)
They're turning. There they go. They're still turning!
They're heading for the tower again!
(*Drops mike, raises telephone.*)

LIEUTENANT

Ten seconds! Nine . . . eight . . . seven . . . six . . . five
. . . four . . . three . . . two . . . one . . . *zero!*
(*During count-down, simultaneously:*)

| POLLARD | BUSH |
|---|---|
| It's all your fault, Eugene! You've never forgiven me for those hazings back at the Point. For thirty years you've been out to get me and now you've wrecked my career! | (*To* KING)<br>It's all your fault, you blundering idiot! How in the name of Creation did you let that plane get off the ground without a radio operator? |

(*As* LIEUTENANT *reaches zero, both* GENERALS' *tirades are cut short by a blinding flash of light and a thunderous explosion. The stage blacks out.*)

(*Pre-dawn sky.* WILL *descends into view swaying from a parachute. He holds* BEN *by the scruff of the neck.*)

BEN

Pull to the left! Pull to the right!

WILL

Hold still, Ben.

136

BEN

What did you do it for? You snatched me right out of the plane! What did you do it for?

WILL

Well, I knowed you done took off your parachute. Heck, you'da done the same for me.

BEN

I wouldn't! Our post was the tail of the plane and nobody told us to quit it!

WILL

But the tail was on fire, Ben. Our post was quittin' us.

BEN

Do you know what we are now?

WILL

We're alive . . .

BEN

*We are deserters!* Deserters!

WILL

Stop wrigglin', Ben. *Please.*

BEN

Here's the first lick of danger and you snatch me away from it! (*Folds arms belligerently*) I'd rather be a dead hero than a live deserter.

137

WILL

(*Pause. Stubbornly*)
I ain't gonna drop you, no matter *what* you say.


BEN

(*Sullenly*)
Out in the middle of no place . . . take us *weeks* to get
back to the base. Can't even see where we are . . .


WILL

Sun'll be up in a few minutes, Ben. Don't worry. (*Pause.
Conversationally*) It's always darkest before the dawn.
 (BEN *squirms disgustedly, putting an end to the talk.*
 WILL *looks at audience, gives an uncomprehending*
 *shrug. Lights fade out.*)

 (*A spotlight appears on* GENERAL BUSH, *standing be-*
 *fore a microphone, downstage near portal. He reads*
 *from a sheet of paper.*)


BUSH

"Ten days ago, in 'Operation Prometheus,' the power of the
atom bomb was challenged by a band of battle-hardened air
aces. When General Pollard and I planned this shining symbol of man's unconquerability we had no idea that the news-
papers would give it so very much publicity. To these brave
volunteers I award the air medal for valor beyond the call of
duty: Lieutenants Bridges, Gardella, Kendall and Cover."
How does it sound, King?
 (KING, *wearing earphones, sticks his head out from be-*
 *hind portal.*)


KING

Very sincere, sir.

BUSH

I just hope I don't choke on their names. When this whole thing quiets down I'm sending those men to Iceland.

KING

Ready to hear the playback?

BUSH

Wait, there's more. (KING *disappears*) "Two did not return. In the shattered tail of the plane, all that remained were two charred helmets and a handful of dust. I ask you now to rise as I award these medals posthumously to the gallant heroes who gave the last measure of devotion, Privates Stackpole and Whitehead."

KING

(*Appearing again*)
Stockdale and Whitledge, sir.

BUSH

(*Squinting at script*)
"Stockdale and Whitledge . . ." This is where the bugler plays Taps, right?

KING

Yes, sir. And the flags go to half-mast.

BUSH

Be sure that second bugler is stationed up in the hills to play the echo.

KING

I'll check on it, sir. (*Martial music is heard*) I'll just rewind the tape and give you the playback.

BUSH

There isn't time. The band has started.

(*Lights come up on* BUSH's *office and anteroom.*)

LIEUTENANT ABEL

(*In office, holding* BUSH's *jacket*)
General Bush! Only five minutes, sir!

> (BUSH *goes upstage into office.* KING *takes microphone
> and exits into wings. In office* CAPTAIN CHARLES *is
> crouching by the radio, busily brushing the visor of*
> BUSH's *garrison cap.* LIEUTENANT BAKER *is looking out
> the window with a pair of binoculars.* BUSH *slips into
> the jacket which* ABEL *is holding for him.*)

BUSH

(*To* CHARLES)
Brush, man, brush! That's genuine leather! (*To* ABEL)
Watch the sleeve there . . .

BAKER

The grandstands are full, sir!

BUSH

You're darn right they are! Those men are on duty. All
leaves were canceled today. (*Mumbling from radio*) What?
What did he say?

CHARLES

Senator Hawk and Senator Winkle are in the reviewing
stand!

BUSH

Good, Good! Baker, bring the car around!

**BAKER**

Yes, sir.
(*Exits.*)

**BUSH**

Abel, check on those reporters!

**ABEL**

Yes, sir.
(*Exits. More mumbling from radio.*)

**BUSH**

What was that? What did he say?

**CHARLES**

General Pollard just came in!

**BUSH**

(*Snatching cap from* CHARLES)
Shut that off! (CHARLES *turns off radio and hurries out.* BUSH
*dons cap, unfurls speech, rehearses*) Two did not return . . .
(BEN *and* WILL *come into the anteroom*) Two did *not* return
. . .

(BEN *moves closer to dividing door, which is open.*
WILL *follows.*)

**BEN**

Excuse me, sir, I—

**BUSH**

Your uniform is *filthy*, boy!

BEN

I know, sir. We hitchhiked some but we had to walk a lot and—

BUSH

You know? And do you know what day this is?

BEN

Saturday, sir. I wanted to—

BUSH

The proudest day in the history of this base, that's all! People have come from miles around—generals, senators—to do homage to two enlisted men, your brothers-in-arms, and you don't even have enough courtesy and respect to put on a decent uniform!

BEN

Sir, please, I want to turn myself in.

WILL

(*Over him*)

He didn't jump, sir! I pulled him out!

BAKER

(*At the door*)

The car is ready, sir.

BUSH

What squadron are you in?

BEN

The Ninth Squadron, sir.

BUSH

The Ninth! Stackpole and Whitehead's own outfit . . . !

WILL AND BEN

(*Coming to attention and saluting*)
Stockdale and Whitledge, sir!

BUSH

Well, whoever they were. By God, you're going to stay
right here until I finish the ceremony and then we'll see if we
can put a little decency and esprit de corps into you! I don't
want our visitors to get even a *glimpse* of you! Dirty uniforms, today of all days!
    (*He exits.* WILL *and* BEN *look at each other, drop sa-
    lutes.*)

WILL

Well, we turned ourselves in. I *think* . . .

BEN

Yeah, wait till he finds out that besides wearing dirty uniforms, we're deserters.
    (BEN *stalks into anteroom.* WILL *follows, closing con-
    necting door.* BEN *sits on bench, grimly snaps up a
    copy of* Time *from adjacent table.*)

WILL

I told him I pulled you out, Ben. I'll tell him again . . .

BEN

Aww . . .
    (BEN *riffles pages of magazine gloomily.* WILL, *watch-
    ing uneasily, sits beside him.* KING *enters office, whis-*

*tling "Flow Gently, Sweet Afton." He flicks radio on,
and martial music is heard.* KING *sits at* GENERAL's *desk.
In anteroom,* WILL *is watching* BEN's *black mood with
concern.)*

WILL

Say, Ben, did I ever tell you the story about the turkey
that got in with a coopful of chickens?

BEN

I don't want to hear it . . .

WILL

You'll enjoy it, Ben . . . You see, this turkey got in with
these chickens—

BEN

I don't want to hear it.

WILL

It's a right good story, Ben.

BEN

Don't you understand, we'll probably be shot!

WILL

Well, then, you don't hear it now, you're likely never to
hear it.

BEN

*(Rising, magazine in hand)*

Oh!

WILL

What's the matter, Ben?

144

BEN

Lieutenant Bridges on the cover.


WILL

I wish you'd look!


VOICE ON RADIO

(*As music fades*)

General Bush has just taken his place on the reviewing stand . . . and now the four Lieutenants who are to receive the Air Medal are bravely mounting the platform.

(KING *is removing his shoes, putting them beside desk.*)


BEN

(*Looking from magazine to radio*)

The Lieutenants are getting medals! They're heroes!


WILL

Gol-ly!


BEN

If we'd stayed on the plane, we would be heroes!


VOICE ON RADIO

It's a solemn moment, ladies and gentlemen; the many visiting dignitaries standing at attention, the flags at half-mast in honor of the two men who gave their lives in "Operation Prometheus," Privates Stockdale and Whitledge . . .


WILL AND BEN

Stockdale and Whitledge?

145

VOICE ON RADIO

Yes, Stockdale and Whitledge! Names that will live as long as men are free!

(*Martial music comes up again.*)

WILL

We *are* heroes, Ben!

BEN

But we ain't dead!

WILL

Well, that makes it even better, don't it?

BEN

They think we're heroes and we're a couple of rotten no-good deserters . . .

WILL

Golly, will they be surprised!
(KING *rises, crosses office.*)

BEN

They'll kill us, that's what they'll do! They'll kill us!
(KING *opens anteroom door, takes magazine from table, closes door, heads back for desk. He stops, looks back at closed door, shakes his head vigorously and continues to desk.*)

WILL

Come on, Ben. They'll be real glad we're alive, you'll see.
(WILL *goes to connecting door, opens it.* BEN *follows.* KING *has his feet up on the desk and the magazine held open before his face.* WILL *and* BEN *enter office*) Howdy, Sergeant!

**BEN**

(*Saluting*)

Private Ben Whitledge reporting for duty after an unforeseen delay, sir!

**WILL**

I'll bet you never expected to see us again, but here we are!

**KING**

(*Slowly lowering magazine*)

No . . . No . . . No . . .

**WILL**

Didn't I tell you he'd be surprised, Ben?

**KING**

Why—ain't—you—dead?

(BEN *remains at petrified attention.*)

**WILL**

No excuse, sir!

**KING**

You ain't dead. . . . You ain't dead . . .

**WILL**

Well, I had my parachute on.

**KING**

. . . and I'm the one who identified your remains. . . . Two charred helmets and a pile of dust . . . they're having a ceremony down there. . . .

BUSH

(*On radio*)
Ten days ago, in "Operation Prometheus," the power of
the atom bomb was challenged by a band of battle-hardened
air aces. When General Pollard and I planned this shining
symbol of man's unconquerability, we had no idea—

WILL

(*Over the above, pointing to radio*)
Is that the General? Is he gonna give us medals?

KING

The General . . . ! (*Flings himself at radio, shuts it off,
beats on it*) Oh, God! Oh, my God!

WILL

Now that ain't no way to act, Sergeant. Here Ben and me
is alive and you—

KING

(*Pushing them into anteroom*)
Medals! He's giving you medals! (*Slamming door on* WILL
*and* BEN, *he rushes from the office*) Lieutenant! Lieutenant!

BEN

We'll be shot. We'll be shot!

WILL

(*Leading* BEN *to the bench*)
No, it's just that he's kind of surprised right now. Later on,
they'll be right happy we're here, you'll see.
(KING *and* ABEL *come running into office.*)

148

#### ABEL

*What?* (KING, *nodding points to door.* ABEL *throws it open.* BEN *snaps to attention*) No . . . No, no . . . Don't move, do you understand, don't move! (*He slams door, then flings it open again*) Don't move or I'll have you shot! (*He slams door again.* BEN *wilts.* ABEL *grabs* KING) You get over to the reviewing stand on the double and tell the General to stop the proceedings. There's radio and television and newsreel cameras there, and if he gives posthumous medals to two men who are standing right here in his own office he'll be the laughing stock of the whole country! Step on it! (KING *runs.* ABEL *flings connecting door open.* BEN *snaps to attention*) Stay away from the windows, you understand? Stay away from the doors! Just don't move! And if anybody comes in here you tell them you're John Jones and Jack Smith, you got that?

#### WILL

Yes, sir!

(ABEL *slams door and mops his brow.* BEN *collapses.*)

#### BEN

They're gonna kill us . . . they're gonna kill us . . .

#### WILL

(*Taking up* Time *and fanning* BEN *with it*)
No they ain't. Breathe deep.

(CHARLES *bursts into office.*)

#### CHARLES

(*To* ABEL)

What the hell's going on here? Sergeant King just jumped an Air Policeman and stole his motorcycle.

**149**

ABEL

The two men who are getting the posthumous medals . . . they're inside.

CHARLES

The medals?

ABEL

The men.

CHARLES

You're drunk.

ABEL

Go ahead, look!

CHARLES

(*Opens connecting door slowly. Peers in.* WILL *turns from his fanning*)

Who are you?

WILL

I'm John Jones and this here is Jack Smith.

CHARLES

(*Slams door*)

Listen, Jim, if you're trying to pull my leg, it'll be the last time, because joking about the dead is carrying it just a little too far.

ABEL

Dead? That's them, right there! That idiot gave those names because I told them to! They're the ones; Sergeant King identified them.

CHARLES

I'm beginning to think that doesn't mean too much! *He identified them once before, didn't he?*

ABEL

(*Snatching newspaper from desk*)
Here's their pictures! You want more proof?

CHARLES

Lord. Lordy Lord . . .
(WILL *stops fanning, looks at back of magazine.*)

WILL

Lieutenant Gardella don't really smoke Camels, does he?
(WILL *resumes fanning.* KING *runs into office.*)

ABEL

Well? Did you stop him in time?

KING

Sir, I reported to the General and informed him as to the situation and advised him that under the very unusual circumstances, as it has been found out that contrary to all Intelligence reports to the contrary, he desist . . .

ABEL

In English, damn it! Had he already presented the medals or not?

KING

Yes sir, he had.

ABEL

Lord!
(*Runs from office.*)

CHARLES

Lordy Lord. What did he say?

KING

He said that—

BUSH

(*A fearful bellow from offstage*)
*I'll court-martial everybody in the whole damn Air Force!*

KING

That's what he said, sir.
(BUSH, *livid, bursts into office.* BAKER *follows him.*)

BUSH

Where are they? Where are they? Where are the two privates who hold my career in the palm of their hands?

CHARLES

In there, sir.
(*Points to door.* BUSH *flings it open and steps into anteroom.* BEN *and* WILL *come to attention and salute.*)

BUSH

You two!

WILL

Yes, sir. We got back here as quick as we could. (*Pause.*
BUSH *stares*) And we sure do appreciate you givin' up medals
and all and settin' the flags at half-mast. (WILL *shakes* BUSH's

*hand.* BUSH *winces sickly)* And I got the whole thing figgered out, sir. I have. You see, before all the excitement started in the plane up there, I was cleanin' and sweepin' in the back. Well, you know that handful of dust Sergeant King was talkin' about? (BUSH *nods dumbly)* That's what it was, a handful of dust. If I'da knowed yall was gonna think it was *us,* I'da swept it under a seat or somethin'! Well, anyhow, what it all comes down to is, we ain't dead!

(BUSH *totters back into office, closing the door.* WILL *lowers* BEN'S *saluting arm and resumes fanning him.* BUSH *stares at* KING.)

#### BUSH

Ten minutes ago, in front of half the brass in the continental United States, I awarded the Air Medal to a pile of dust. Do you know what this is going to do to me, Sergeant King, when this story gets out?

#### KING

Sir, I didn't know that they were—

#### BUSH

For thirty-two years I've been building a reputation! For dignity, for responsibility, for coolness in the crisis and clear-thinking in the clutch! Tomorrow I will probably be known throughout the entire Pentagon as "Old Dustpan!"

#### KING

Sir, there were these two charred helmets and this—

#### BUSH

I am not interested in how you *knew* these men in there were dead, Sergeant King! You are responsible for this whole mess!

KING

(*Saluting rapidly*)

Yes, sir! Yes, sir!

ABEL

(*Entering office*)

The reporters, sir! They're on their way over. They want to know why you ran out in the middle of Taps.

BUSH

Stall them! Keep them away! Show them the new gymnasium! (ABEL *exits*) I've got to get those men off my base. If anybody sees them—if anybody hears them—

KING

You could transfer them to another base, sir—

BUSH

Shut up! . . . What? Of course! (*To* CHARLES) Go down to the basement and get as many DD–613 forms as you can lay your hands on.

CHARLES

You mean DAF 39-J, don't you, sir?

BUSH

I mean DD-613! (CHARLES *exits.* BUSH *calls after him*) Well, if you find any DAF-39-J's . . . (*To* BAKER) You. Go get a car and bring it around back. Quietly. See if you can find one of those old jobs, with window shades.

BAKER

Yes, sir!

(*Exits.*)

**BUSH**

You!

**KING**

*(Saluting, heading for door)*

Yes, sir!

**BUSH**

The phone. Get through to General Hooper, down in Texas. See if he's got room for a couple of new privates on his base. Bright, hardworking boys.

**KING**

Yes, sir.
   *(Goes to phone.)*

**BUSH**

But first get those miserable men in here!

**KING**

Yes, sir.
   *(Heads for anteroom)*

**BUSH**

And put your shoes on!

**KING**

Yes, sir.
   *(Snatches shoes from floor, opens anteroom door and beckons* WILL *and* BEN *into office.* KING *returns to telephone.* WILL *and* BEN *enter office hesitantly.* BUSH *draws himself up, glares at them, then melts into a department-store-Santa-Claus chuckle.)*

**BUSH**

Ha-ha-ha-ho-ho-ho. Well, it looks like we're had a little mix-up, boys, doesn't it?

**WILL**

Yes sir, it sure do.

**BUSH**

*It sure do,* all right, ha-ha-ha-ho-ho. But I guess we can straighten it out, can't we? You can straighten most things out if everybody co-operates. That's all it takes, just a little cooperation isn't that so? Ha-ha-ha.

**BEN**

*(Through chattering teeth)*
Yes, sir, yes, sir, yes, sir, yes, sir . . .

**BUSH**

Well, I'm mighty glad to hear you feel that way about it, because if you didn't there could be all kinds of trouble! You boys could even get court-martialed and you wouldn't like that, would you? Ha-ha-ha. No sir, that's the reason we're—

**BEN**

Give it to us, sir! We deserve it!

**BUSH**

No, no, no, we're just going to co-operate and everything will—

**BEN**

We deserted when we should've stuck to our posts!

BUSH

Well, accidents will happen, and sometimes—

BEN

Throw the book at us, sir!

BUSH
(*To* WILL)
What's the matter with *him*?

WILL

He's worryin' he ain't dead.

BUSH

Oh, for pity's sake!

BEN

I plead guilty, sir. There was no excuse, sir.

ABEL
(*Entering*)
The reporters, sir. They've seen the gymnasium and they still want to see *you*.

BUSH

Oh, no . . .

BEN

I'll make a full confession, sir!

BUSH

No! Don't let them in. Tell them I'm sick. Tell them I've gone home.
(ABEL *exits.*)

157

BAKER

(*Entering through anteroom*)

I've got the car, sir.

BUSH

Good! Good! Get rid of this idiot!

BEN

(*As* BAKER *hustles him out*)

The Universal Code of Military Justice says that a soldier who deserts his post should be tried by court-martial!

BUSH

(*Calling after them*)

Lock him in!

WILL

Sir, listen—

BUSH

Get into that car out there.

WILL

Sir, listen, I don't want you to give Ben no punishment. It's my fault he warn't killed, not his'n.

BUSH

Now *look*, nobody's going to punish anybody! I'm just going to transfer the two of you to another air base, that's all! Now will you please get into that car?

WILL

(*Snapping his fingers*)

Sir, as long as you're fixin' to transfer us, couldn't it please be into the Infantry?

BUSH

No, no! I said I wasn't going to punish you and I meant it!

WILL

But it's where we *want* to go, sir!

BUSH

Out of the question! Airmen can *not* transfer into the Infantry. Now if you don't get into that car before someone sees you, so help me Hannah, I'm going to have you court-martialed!

WILL

(*Starts to go, then stops*)
Excuse me for sayin' it, sir, but if you done that a whole lot of people would see me, wouldn't they?

BUSH

What! . . . (*Dazed, turns slowly to* KING. *Softly*) Every bit of this is your fault, Sergeant. If you hadn't sent that plane up with this nincompoop at the radio—

KING

(*Rising, covering mouthpiece of phone*)
Me, sir? *My* fault! Now look, sir—

BUSH

Stockdale, be reasonable! I'll find an air base right near your home! That would make you happy, wouldn't it?

WILL

I'm sorry, sir, but if Ben and me can't go into the Infantry I reckon we're better off staying right here.

KING

Will, what do you want to upset the General for? The Infantry's murder. Believe me.

WILL

Ben had a chance to go and he tore it up. You know that.

KING

I'll give you back the watch, Will.

BUSH

I'll give you mine too.

WILL

I'm sorry, sir. The Infantry's what we want.
(BUSH *and* KING *look at each other.* KING *becomes conscious of phone in his hand, hangs up.* ABEL *enters.*)

ABEL

The reporters are *here,* sir.

BUSH

You're asking the impossible, Stockdale! It would take an Act of Congress! Absolutely impossible!

(*Blackout—except for a spot on* WILL. *He grins, comes downstage and addresses audience.*)

WILL

Now *you* know, when you put your mind to it there ain't *nothin'* impossible. General Bush, he got them reporters in there and told 'em all about how it was such a proud day in the history of the base and all like that, and then the reporters left and him and Sergeant King let me out of the closet . . . And then General Pollard come over and him and General Bush talked some . . . argued, you might say . . . well, what it was was cussin'. All I said to General Pollard was "Howdy" and he knowed who I was right off. He did. Then he left and the next thing you know, me and Sergeant King and General Bush was all pilin' into this great big car. With window shades. And did we drive! Till after dark and then some. And all the time General Bush kept mumblin' to hisself. After a while I made out what he was mumblin'. He was sayin' over and over again, "Where there's a will, there's a way." I asked him to stop, 'cause it's right embarrassin' to hear someone praisin' you like that. Well, finally we was done drivin', and I could tell by the smell of the pines and the sound of the frogs we was out in the woods. Just then the moon come up and things commenced to happen.

(*Spot on* WILL *blacks out, and lights dim up on a clearing in the woods. The rear end of an* AIR FORCE *sedan projects onstage right. There is a tent upstage, with its side rolled up. Within the tent, a* CORPORAL *sits typing by lantern light.* WILL *steps back into the scene and watches as* KING *gives orders to a line of armed sentries.*)

### KING

All right, have you got it straight now? Challenge everybody. The password is "Nightmare." If they don't give it, *shoot!* Okay—sentries, take your posts. On the double!
(SENTRIES *trot off in various directions.* BUSH *enters, followed by* ABEL, BAKER *and* CHARLES, *who go into tent.*)

BUSH

Are you sure we've got the whole area surrounded?

KING

I think so, sir. Tell you the truth, I've never done anything like this before.

BUSH

Do you think I have? Guns. Passwords . . .

WILL

It sure is excitin', ain't it?

BUSH

Look, you just stand over there and let me handle this. Please! (*To* KING) Where's General Pollard?

KING

On his way, sir.

BUSH

Are the forms ready for him to sign?

KING

The corporal's working on them, sir.
(*An approaching car is heard from the left.*)

BUSH

Well, speed him up! That must be Pollard's car now.

KING

Yes, sir.
(*Goes to tent.*)

162

SENTRY
*(Off)*

Halt! Give the password!
*(Silence, then a volley of shots ring out.)*

BUSH

Great Scott, they've shot Pollard!

POLLARD
*(Off)*

Eugene! Tell these idiots to stop shooting! It's me! Vernon!
*(Another shot.)*

BUSH

Give the password!

POLLARD
*(Off)*

I've forgotten the damn thing.

BUSH

Nightmare!

WILL

Nightmare!
*(Another shot.)*

POLLARD
*(Off)*

Nightmare, goddammit! (*He storms into the clearing, brandishing a shooting stick*) Look here, Eugene, you're carrying this thing just a little too far!

**BUSH**

I'm sorry, Vernon, the sentries are as nervous as I am.
(*There is loud hammering from the trunk of the sedan.*
BUSH *and* POLLARD *throw up their arms.*)

**BUSH AND POLLARD**

Nightmare!

**BUSH**

It's the other dead hero, Vernon. The talkative one. I hid
him in the trunk for total security.

**WILL**

Ben's in the trunk?
(*More hammering.*)

**BUSH**

All right, Stockdale. Get the keys and let him out.
(WILL *goes around car for keys.*)

**POLLARD**

Listen, Eugene, we could both get into a hell of a lot of
trouble, pulling a deal like this.

**BUSH**

We are in trouble, Vernon. Clear up to our pensions. Now
come on, sign those papers.
(*They go up to tent.* WILL *unlocks trunk of car, raises
lid.* BEN *sticks his head out, peers around.*)

**WILL**

Howdy, Ben!

164

BEN

I knew it . . . they got us out in no-man's land . . .

WILL

(*Helping him out*)
Come on . . . here you go . . .

BEN

Good-bye, Will.

WILL

We just now got here, Ben.

BEN

And we ain't never going back. Will, I know you didn't do it on purpose and I know there wasn't no meanness behind it. (*Extends hand*) I forgive you.

WILL

(*Shaking hands*)
You mean we're buddies again?

BEN

For a little while . . .

KING

(*Coming down from tent*)
All right, Whitledge, you're first. Sentry! Take him inside. See that he signs everything in triplicate.
(*A* SENTRY *drags* BEN *up to the tent.*)

BEN

'Bye, Will.

165

WILL

'Bye, Ben. (*To* KING) Golly, is he gonna be surprised!

KING

We can say good-bye too, Will.

WILL

I'm sure gonna miss you, Sergeant!

KING

Me too. I could hardly type your transfers for the tears in my eyes.

WILL

You know—everyone's all the time sayin' how sergeants is mean and tough, so I'm right glad you was my first one. You showed me different.

KING

Thanks, Will. (*They shake hands.* WILL *looks at* KING's *watch*) Okay, I'm going to give you the watch anyway. Here. Go on, take it.

WILL

Gee, I never held that against you . . .

KING

(*Backing away*)

We're square now. I don't owe you nothing; you don't owe me nothing. We're square.

(BUSH *and* POLLARD *come down from tent.*)

BUSH

King, what's the matter with that Whitledge? He keeps saying he's sorry he has only one life to give for his country.
(KING *makes crazy sign, goes up to tent.*)

WILL

He figgers you brought us here to get shot, sir.

BUSH AND POLLARD

Shot?
(*They look at each other speculatively.*)

BUSH

Ridiculous . . . All these witnesses, Vernon . . . (POLLARD *returns to tent.* BUSH *flourishes a clipboard*) All right, Stockdale, I've just got a couple of letters for you to sign and then we'll be through with this mess. This one is to your folks, saying that you're on a very important secret mission, and this one certifies that you've never heard of "Operation Prometheus" and have never been on my base in your entire life. Sign here.
(*Shoves pen at* WILL.)

WILL

But if we never heard of "Operation Whatchamacallit," then we don't get no medals, do we?

BUSH

Medals! Of course not! Sign here . . .

WILL

Ben sets a lot of stock in medals and all like that.

BUSH

Now look—you just sign these letters! You're going into the Infantry; what more do you want?

WILL

But if we don't sign, then we're still dead—and Ben's medal will be sent to his folks and he could just go home and pick it up, couldn't he?

BUSH

Well, yes . . . well, no! . . . well . . .

WILL

Looks to me like we're *best* off just stayin' dead!

BUSH

You can't *do* that! All right, all right. (*Detaches a ribbon from his jacket*) Here's a ribbon. Now sign.

WILL

This way is okay for me, sir, but couldn't you do it up right for Ben?

BUSH

Do it up—

WILL

You know, give him a real medal, not just a little ribbon. And everybody standin' up stifflike and you sayin' a whole lot of words.

BUSH

You want me to *present* a medal . . . out here in the woods . . . in the middle of the night?

168

**WILL**

That's right! We'll get everybody standin' up over there, and we could turn some of the cars around so their lights is shinin'! Maybe we can get some music on the radio! Hey, driver, could you turn that car around!

(*Runs off right.*)

**BUSH**

No! No! I don't have any medals!

**POLLARD**

(*Coming down from tent*)
How long is this going to take, Eugene?

**BUSH**

(*Caling after* WILL)
I didn't bring any medals!

**POLLARD**

I want to get to bed.

**BUSH**

(*Turning to the be-medaled* POLLARD)
I don't have any med— Ohhh . . . !

**POLLARD**

What are you staring at?

**BUSH**

Vernon . . . old man . . . I wonder if you could give me . . . one of your . . . medals?

**POLLARD**

What?

**BUSH**

Just one, Vernon! You've got so many of them!

**POLLARD**

What are you talking about, Eugene?

**BUSH**

Stockdale wants a medal!

**POLLARD**

To hell with him!

**BUSH**

No! Vernon, if you give me one of yours . . . I'll give you *two* of mine. I swear I will.

**POLLARD**

But these medals are sewn on!

**BUSH**

Sewn?
>           (WILL *re-enters, approaches them.*)

**POLLARD**

Yes, dammit!

**BUSH**
>           (*To* WILL, *pleadingly*)
His medals are *sewn* on . . .

### WILL

I got my mumbly-peg knife.
(*Producing it.*)

### BUSH

(*Handing* POLLARD *the knife*)
A small one, Vernon . . . Please . . .

### POLLARD

(*Snatching knife*)
I'll do this in private, if you don't mind!
(POLLARD *storms off into the trees. From the right, a pair of headlight beams swing around, and an orchestra playing "Goody, Goody" is heard.*)

### BUSH

There's nothing else you can think of at the moment, is there, Stockdale? You do understand why we don't have a brass band, don't you?

### WILL

I wouldn't worry about it none. This'll do fine. I'll just get the fellows lined up. Hey, Corporal! (CORPORAL *comes out of tent.* WILL *salutes*) Howdy. Would you please go over there and stand up at attention, real smart-like.

### CORPORAL

Do what?

### BUSH

Just do as you're told! On the double!

WILL

Captain, could you and the Lieutenants come out here a minute, please? (CHARLES, BAKER *and* ABEL *emerge from tent.* WILL *salutes*) Howdy. Would you fellows go over there with the Corporal and stand up at attention, please?

THREE OFFICERS

DO WHAT?

BUSH

Get over there! You ought to know enough to obey orders by now!
> (POLLARD *storms back on, the front of his jacket slashed and torn. He thrusts a medal at* BUSH.)

POLLARD

I've been blackmailed, I've been shanghaied, I've been shot at, and now I've been robbed.

WILL

Boy, Ben's gonna pop his shirt when both you Generals snap to attention!

POLLARD

DO WHAT?

BUSH

Vernon, please . . .

POLLARD

Never! Not on your life!
> (*Flips open his shooting stick and sits on it.*)

172

BUSH

*I'll* stand at attention! I'll stand on my head! Please sign!

WILL

(*Taking pen*)
Clean forgot! Last name first, first name, middle name last?

BUSH

Just your regular signature. (SENTRIES *enter*) You men get over there with the others!
(SENTRIES *join group standing at attention*.)

WILL

I'll go fetch Ben.
(WILL *exits into tent as* KING *emerges, a sheaf of papers in his hand.*)

BUSH

King, have you got those orders?

KING

Yes, sir.

BUSH

(*Calling to tent*)
All right, dammit, come out and get it!

WILL

(*Leading* BEN *out*)
Go ahead, Ben. Strut right up to the General and he's gonna give you somethin'.

BEN

I know. Good-bye, Will.

BUSH

King . . .

KING

(*Reading*)
"The following enlisted men are hereby relieved of duty
and removed from the records of Major General Eugene
Bush, and transferred to the command of Major General
Vernon I. Pollard, U.S. Army, Infantry."

BEN

What?

WILL

We're in the Infantry, Ben.

BEN

The Infantry?

WILL

You finally made it, Ben.

BEN

Oh, no . . . oh, golly . . . oh. . . .

KING

(*Crossing and handing papers to them*)
Private Benjamin B. Whitledge . . . Private Will Stockdale . . . So long, boys. It's been swell knowing you!

WILL AND BEN

So long, Sergeant.

KING

Wish I could go along with you, but that's life!

WILL
(To BUSH)
Gee, couldn't he, sir? Go along with us?

BUSH

Brilliant idea, Stockdale! Vernon?

POLLARD

Wonderful!

KING

No, no, no—

WILL
(Throwing his arm around KING's shoulder)
We're still gonna be together!

BEN

In the Infantry!

KING

What happened?

BUSH

Detail, atten-shun!

POLLARD
(Sitting with his arms folded)
Damned if I'll stand at attention!

VOICE ON RADIO

. . . broadcasting on 1200 kilocycles. Good night.
(*Drum roll.*)

BUSH

It gives me great pleasure to award this medal which through a regrettable error was previously awarded post-humously, to Private Benjamin B. Whitledge, U.S. Army, Infantry.

(*Band on radio plays "The Star-Spangled Banner."* POLLARD *leaps to attention and salutes.* BEN *marches up to* BUSH *to receive his medal.* WILL *comes downstage and addresses audience as "Meeting Hall" curtain falls and the scene behind it slowly fades out.*)

WILL

Everythin' come out as good as Tony and the Pony, didn't it? Well, that's how I got my ribbon and Ben got his medal, and how us Three Musketeers wound up in the Infantry after all. I want to thank yall for bein' such good listeners and not leavin' the hall no more'n you had to. Mrs. Calhoun got her shoe back? Good. Well, I guess I better quit now, because—(*Looks carefully at watch*)—Mickey Mouse got his hands way up to goin' home time! Good night! Good night!

(*He runs off into the wings.*)

*Curtain*

# Date Due